CHHATRAPATI SAMBHAJI MAHARAJ

AN INVINCIBLE KING

SUJIT NAMDEV TAMBE

"Dedicated to the Rajmata Jijausaheb, the Great
Chhatrapati Shivaji Maharaj & Protector of Swarajya
the Great Dharmaveer Chhatrapati Sambhaji
Maharaj"

॥ जय जिजाऊ जय शिवराय जय शंभुराजे ॥

Sujit Namdev Tambe

In the remembrance of King Dharmaveer
Chhatrapati Sambhaji Maharaj
(14 May 1657 - 11 March 1689)

Sujit Namdev Tambe

Author's Message

Awakening the spark of Swarajya from the corners of the mountains of Sahyadri, Chhatrapati Shivaji Maharaj had taught his successors and chiefs the lessons of waving his life for Swarajya. Chhatrapati Sambhaji Maharaj was no exception; he had the skills of self-government and bravery in his blood. Chhatrapati Sambhaji Maharaj's place in history as a mighty king and skilled organizer is still intact today as Chhatrapati Sambhaji Raje lived his life fearlessly embracing death till his last breath. After Chhatrapati Shivaji Maharaj, Shambhuraje had managed the Swarajya very well.

It is said that Chhatrapati Sambhaji Maharaj was more powerful than Chhatrapati Shivaji Maharaj in terms of aggression. He always tried to protect the Swarajya as well as expand it. It is recorded that Chhatrapati Sambhaji Maharaj fought about 140+ wars during his career. However, they did not lose a single battle. Chhatrapati Sambhaji Raje's method of marching on the enemy was stormy. They were never captured by the enemy, but were captured by their own people. Otherwise, Shambhu Raje would be a storm which is impossible to control! We will experience this history in English with the effect of the war waged by Siddhi, the Britishers, the Portuguese, the Mughals, the Chikkadevarais and own people against him. The biggest challenge for Chhatrapati Sambhaji Maharaj was to recreate the broken-down Swarajya on new lines. He attempted to join Maratha society on a profound premise as well as based on strong military and regulatory forces.

Charges against Chhatrapati Sambhaji Maharaj which alluded to him as womanizer and alcohol inclined stand wrong on the grounds that no single paper is accessible about his rowdiness subsequent to assuming responsibility for the state.

He was never flippant and never silly in his political choices. He has pushed back the Portuguese down and extended Maratha realms into Karnataka. Chhatrapati Sambhaji's endeavors and his last penance prompted the strong establishment of Swarajya even after his passing for the next two centuries up to 1818. His capacities as a warrior, general, and ruler were generally presented to society.

The Portuguese papers have portrayed Chhatrapati Sambhaji as a warlike Prince, which implies he had confronted wars and battled with unfriendly conditions, which lead to the ascent of sparkling stars in the historical course of time. The one who considers Chhatrapati Sambhaji Maharaj as their role model should enjoy reading. Everyone should keep in mind that the Chhatrapati Sambhaji Maharaj's first identity is an undefeated warrior after winning more than 140 battles on the battlefield and the second identity as a Sanskrit Pandit by writing books like Budhbhushan, Satsatak, Nakhshik and Nayikabhed. If you want an inspiration as a writer, only a king like Chhatrapati Sambhaji Maharaj can inspire you in this world.

King Shambhu is the inspiration for survival,

King Shambhu is the strength to cope with any crisis,

King Shambhu is the ray of hope in the darkness,

King Shambhu is the focus of life,

King Shambhu is the energy to achieve the goal,

Every breath of mine is King Shambhu.

- Sujit Namdev Tambe

Acknowledgement

I would like to mention here that, this book was impossible without support from my beloved ones.

I specially wanted to thank my Father (Namdev Popatrao Tambe) & Mother (Jayashree Namdev Tambe) for all the support throughout this journey of writing the book. As they were aware about how much affection was there in me for Chhatrapati Sambahji Maharaj. They literally insisted me to study Chhatrapati Sambhaji Maharaj's life. With their Love & Support, I started reading about King Shambhu & studied some aspects on which I focused in this book specially.

Also, I wanted to express my gratitude towards my wife Snehal Sujit Tambe. She helped me a lot in this journey of second edition of this book.

A special thanks to my friends & colleagues for believing in me for what I was doing in the period of time.

Contents

Prologue

Epilogue

Prologue

The Maratha Empire was ruling Delhi. The lessons of betting one's life on Swarajya were instilled in the heirs and chiefs of Chhatrapati Shivaji Maharaj who awakened the spark of Swarajya from the corners of Sahyadri hills. Chhatrapati Sambhaji Maharaj was also born with the skills of self-government and bravery in his blood.

Ever since Chhatrapati Shivaji Maharaj and Chhatrapati Sambhaji Maharaj, who was imprisoned by Aurangzeb, based on treachery, escaped from the Agra and gave trumpets to Aurangzeb, Aurangzeb was planning to conquer the entire Maratha Empire.

After the death of Chhatrapati Shivaji Maharaj at the age of 50, Chhatrapati Sambhaji Maharaj succeeded to the throne as the successor of Chhatrapati Shivaji Maharaj. Chhatrapati Sambhaji Maharaj did not hand over any fort to Aurangzeb. So Aurangzeb was living in the fire of hatred. That is why he had warned his army that he would not get peace unless Chhatrapati Sambhaji Maharaj was captured. Mughal emperor Aurangzeb put down his crown till the date Chhatrapati Sambhaji Maharaj was captured by the Mughal army.

During the range of 9 years of rule Chhatrapati Sambhaji's characteristics, for example, innovativeness, exactness, straight imposition and cautiousness in an organization, and so on are reflected through the archives. Subsequently accuses set forth against him in the later Bakhars composed during the time of Chhatrapati Rajaram can't be acknowledged.

The gallant battle made by Chhatrapati Sambhaji Maharaj against the Mughals intrusion has made a perpetual spot throughout the entire existence of Marathas.

The inferior methodology of history in this way demonstrates another point to take a gander at Chhatrapati Sambhaji Maharaj. The sovereign who battled against Portuguese, British, Siddhi, and Mughal was a valiant trooper and compelling general.

The initiative of Chhatrapati Sambhaji Maharaj has given an incredible arrangement to society. He proceeded with his subjects like a father and he was making each move to follow the reformist strategies of his father Chhatrapati Shivaji Maharaj, the extraordinary. The subject was minded such a lot that a sensation of value was brought appropriately. The methodology of Maharashtra State was agreeable in securing society for example Maharashtra dharma.

The place of Chhatrapati Sambhaji Maharaj in history as a mighty king, the organizer is still intact today as Chhatrapati Sambhaji Raje lived his life as he fearlessly embraced death. After Chhatrapati Shivaji Maharaj, Shambhu Raje held the reins of Swarajya very competently. He always tried to expand his self-government. Using guerrilla tactics, he literally fought, routed, and defeated his enemies.

Chapter I

14 MAY 1657

In the 16th century, Maharashtra was ravaged by tyrannical Adilshahi, Nizamshahi, Qutubshahi and Mughalshahi. India was enslaved for many years. 19 February 1630 was the day; it was as if the sun had been born to erase the darkness of slavery. Chhatrapati Shivaji Maharaj established Swarajya. The people of swarajya had got a rightful basis. When Chhatrapati Shivaji Maharaj said that he will be there for their companion, everyone was relieved. Swarajya was running smoothly.

Chhatrapati Shivaji Maharaj was married to Saibai Maharanisaheb. One day everyone got good news, Swarajya got Prince. Just as Rudra is there to support Shiva, so Shambhu came to support Shivaji.

Chhatrapati Shivaji Maharaj and Saibai had a son on 14 May 1657. There was joy everywhere. It was as if a festival was being celebrated in Swarajya. When the question arose as to what to name the child, Chhatrapati Shivaji Maharaj and Rajmata Jijau named him Sambhaji.

Sambhaji was named after Chhatrapati Shivaji's elder brother. "Sambhaji" "Sambhaji" was hailed everywhere to celebrate the joy of prince.

As a prince, he had learnt the basics of campaigning and politics from an early age. Chhatrapati Sambhaji Maharaj's mother, Maharani Saibai died when Shambhu Raje was 2 years old. After that, Dharau Gade Patil of Kapurhol village near Pune took care of Shambhu Raje as a mother.

Also, Shambhu Raje was taken care of by his grandmother Rajmata Jijau. Maharani Putlabai also cared for him from his childhood.

Shiv-Pratap

Sultan Adilshah of Bijapur died on 1 November 1656. This created an atmosphere of anarchy in Bijapur. Taking advantage of this situation, Aurangzeb attacked Bijapur and Shivaji Raje attacked him instead of supporting Aurangzeb. As a result, Aurangzeb became angry with Shivaji Raje.

And on the orders of Shah Jahan, Aurangzeb made a treaty with Bijapur. During this time, Shah Jahan fell ill. Hence Aurangzeb went back to North India.

Sultan Adilshah II of Bijapur also breathed a sigh of relief after Aurangzeb returned to Agra. Now Shivaji Raje was the most powerful enemy of Bijapur. The Sultan asked Shahaji Raje to keep his son under control. But Shahaji had expressed his inability to do this. Shivaji must be stopped; Begum asked the court and challenged all her chiefs by asking who would stop Shivaji.

No one was getting ready. Afzal Khan took a foot forward to kill Shivaji Raje and he marched on the Marathi Swarajya with a large army. To end Shivaji Raje, Begum sent Afzal Khan (Abdullah Bhatari) against Shivaji Raje.

Afzal Khan traveled in 1659 with a huge army equipped with gunpowder and horsemen. Afzal reached Pratapgad looting on the way. Shivaji Raje was very angry but he knew that his military capability was limited. Therefore, he introduced diplomacy and kept silent.

Afzal Khan was the architect of the arrest of his father Shahaji Raje and the death of his elder brother Sambhaji. Afzal Khan sent a message of friendship with his envoy Krishnaji Bhaskar to Shivaji Raje for negotiation.

Through this, he sent the message that, if Shivaji Raje accepted the orders of Bijapur, the Sultan will give him the right to all the areas which were under Shivaji's control. At the same time, Shivaji Raje will get an honored position in the court of Bijapur.

Shivaji's ministers and advisors were in favor of this treaty. But Shivaji Raje did not like this thing. He gave proper respect to Krishnaji Bhaskar, kept it in his court, and sent his messenger Pant Gopinath Bokil to Afzal Khan to examine the situation. Shivaji Raje felt from Gopinath and Krishnaji Bhaskar that Afzal Khan wanted to arrest him for plotting the treaty.

Shivaji Raje also sent a valuable gift to Afzal Khan while giving his answer to diplomacy. And in this way, Afzal Khan agreed to a treaty.

While preparing for himself, he shortened his long beard. He wore an armor hat on his head. He hides the bichwa(weapon) in his left hand, he puts a new belt in his sleeve, rubs it on his feet, and tightens it. With such strength, Shivaji Raje was ready to come under the fort.

As soon as Afzal Khan approached the Sadar, he was surprised to see the shamiana. Khan sent a message to meet the Shivaji Raje early. Shivaji Raje had come down from the fort. Jiva Mahala came along with Shivaji Raje. The bodyguard of Afzal Khan Sayyad Banda was standing with Khan. Jiva Mahala went towards the shamiana with Shivaji Raje.

On 10 November 1659 Afzal Khan reached the negotiating point with his army. The patriotic comrades who loved Shivaji Maharaj were very concerned about the safety of Shivaji Raje. But in the heart of Shivaji Raje, it was decided to strengthen Swarajya. Shivaji wore his crate, Bakhtiar, kurta, and tunic.

He wore a cap on his head, wore a cap, wore a Vaghnakh (Tigers claws) in one hand, and went to meet Afzal Khan.

The hypocrite Afzal Khan invited Shivaji Raje to hug him. Afzal Khan, a man with a long body, was about to hit the stomach by pressing the neck of Shivaji, who reached the shoulder in his armpit, in a moment, Shivaji tore Khan's stomach from the Vaghnakh hidden in his left hand and killed him. Here Syed Banda, the bodyguard of the Khan, came with a move on the Raje.

Just as he was about to strike, Jiva Mahala cut off Syed Banda's hand and saved Raje. From that incident, one quote is famous in Marathi होता जीवा म्हणून वाचला शिवा.

As soon as the hint of the death of Afzal Khan was ready, the standing Mavali army attacked Khan's army under the leadership of Moropant Pingale and Netaji Palkar; and defeated the army in open war. And the goods Afzal Khan looted while coming to Pratapgad, he took into his possession.

Rajmata Jijau

After killing Afzal Khan, Sambhaji Kavji Kondhalkar placed the head of Khan at the feet of Jijau. Jijau asked him to place it into the main gate of Rajgad. Little Shambhu Raje asked whose head it was, and then Shivaji Raje said it was Khan's head. Then Shambhu Raje asked who is Khan? Shivaji laughed and said that Khan was a bad person, he needed to be destroyed, and he was dangerous for Swarajya. Seeing this incident, everyone started looking at Shambhu with curiosity. Jijau was now happier to see the victory of Maratha Kingdom.

As a childhood of Shambhu Raje, Rajmata Jijau Ma Saheba treated him very well. She told the stories of Ramayana and Mahabharata to young Shambhu Raje. The Shambhu Raje took small lessons from every story that Rajmata Jijau had taught him. He also heard the stories of his grandfather Shahaji Raje and his father Shivaji Raje from Rajmata Jijau and learned them.

One day someone asked Shambhu Raje which is the holy place in this Swarajya?

On this the Shambhu Raje placed their heads at the feet of Rajmata Jijau and said that this is the holy place in the Swarajya. Shambhu Raje learned politics at an early age under the guidance of Jijau.

Going to Agra at the age of 9 is an example of this toughness taught by Rajmata Jijau. Apart from the political learnings, he wrote the books at the age of 14, Budhbhushanam, Nayikabhed, and Nakhshikha & Satsatak.

Treaty of Purandar

During the treaty of Purandar, it was agreed by Shivaji Raje to surrender 23 forts to Mughal emperor Aurangzeb. It was unknown to all that, one more condition was thereby Mirza Raja Jaisingh. It was mentioned that Shambhu Raje should live in the Mughal camp till all forts surrendered. Shivaji Maharaj with a very heavy heart agreed to this & sent 9-year-old Shambhu Raje to Mughal camp.

Diler Khan Pathan along with Raja Jaisingh took Shambhu Raje in their camp.

When Shambhu Raje returned, Diler khan gave him an elephant as a gift and asked,

'How can you take such a big elephant to the Deccan?

Then Shambhu Raje said,

'We will take the elephants anyway, but we are thinking of how to take back the forts given by our Abasaheb (Father).'

At that time a small child leaves Diler Khan clueless.

Understood so many languages

According to many historical records, Shambhu Raje was very handsome and brave. He was also a scholar of many languages and a brilliant politician. He had mastered every part of politics. They got the education along with weapons.

He had also learned so many foreign languages. They were easily trading with the French and English.

Once one English tourist wanted help from the people of Raigad, but Chhatrapati Shivaji Maharaj was not present at that time on the fort. The tourist doesn't understand the Marathi language & Marathi people were not able to decode his English language. There was only one person who can talk with him & the person was Prince Shambhu Raje. Shambhu Raje came in front of English tourists. The man who wanted help asked Shambhu Raje,

Who are you?

Shambhu Raje replied, Sambhaji Prince Sambhaji.

After talking with Sambhaji Raje, the visitor tourist felt very lucky and happy. He gave a salute to Prince Sambhaji. Swarajya got such a great prince; this was the destiny of Swarajya.

Took Expeditions at early age

As a Prince, he undertook many expeditions. Athni was a town near Bijapur. Adilshahi ruled there. The ruler Babbar Khan was very deceitful and monstrous. He was kidnapping women, children, and girls from a nearby village. He had good relations with Arabs; he was selling local women and girls to those people. The transport was carried in the ship by sea. As soon as this news reached the Shambhu Raje, they get angry and he directly attacked Athni with fewer troops.

As soon as Babbar Khan found out about this, he tightened the security guards. However, Shambhu Raje disguised himself and entered the city, and captured Babbar Khan. Hundreds of children, women, and children were released. Yuvraj Shambhu Raje ordered that if anyone oppressed women in the Swarajya, they would be severely punished.

Fight with Lion

There are some such incidents in the pages of history. On their way back from the expedition, the army saw a Lion calf, which they picked up and placed on the side of the road. When the calves were heard crying, the lion ran to that side. 4-5 Marathas resisted her, and then a male Lion came there. He, however, harms Maratha's army.

Prince Shambhu Raje who was coming from behind came to know about this, he jumped directly on the lion to save the life of Maratha. The people who were watching just kept looking; the Shambhu Raje Attacked on lion & the lion's jaw was torn.

" सिंहाच्या जबड्यात घालुनी हात,
मोजिले दात ही मर्द मराठ्यांची जात "

Chapter II

SHIV SHAMBHU

Fighting against the vast Mughal army with courage and extraordinary bravery, Chhatrapati Sambhaji Maharaj was also well versed in literature and Sanskrit. Chhatrapati Sambhaji Maharaj wrote the Sanskrit book Budhbhushan-Rajniti at the age of fourteen. Budhbhushan mentions his father Chhatrapati Shivaji Raje in a very beautiful and figurative language

कलिकालभुजंगमावलीढं निखिलं धर्मवेक्ष्य विक्लवं यः

जगतः पतिरंशतोवतापोः (तीर्णः) स शिवछत्रपतिजयत्यजेयः

In the form of Kaliyuga, this Mughal is sitting on the earth like a snake. Just as Lord Vishnu, who nourishes the world, has to be incarnated to save it, so today Chhatrapati Shivaji Maharaj has conquered and liberated the earth from these tyrants.

Visit to Agra

During the visit to Agra, Shambhu Raje learned a lot from politics. Chhatrapati Shivaji Maharaj took him on his visit to Agra, thinking that if he knew the events and politics of the Mughal court at an early age, it would be useful to him in the future. Shambhu Raje was 9 years old at that time.

Once Aurangzeb asked Shambhu Raje in Agra court,

'Sambhaji go and play a wrestling game with our servants.'

Shambhu Raje denied his order very politely. He said,

'I will play, but the opposite player should be matched to my level. It's up to me, to play or not.' Aurangzeb was shocked. Because no one even dares to talk with him & Shambhu Raje were talking very fearlessly with an eye-to-eye contact.

Aurangzeb asked,

'Don't you fear anyone?'

9-year-old Shambhu Raje smiled & replied,

'I am not afraid of anyone but maybe others are afraid of me.' Aurangzeb was speechless after listening to this answer.

Background of Incident

In March 1665, Shivaji Raje had reached Gokarna Mahabaleshwar after completing the first expedition of Maratha Armor. Maratha's spies brought definite news. Mirza Raja Jaisingh was coming towards Swarajya with an army of lakhs.

That's why Shivaji Raje reached Rajgad in a hurry. The troops from Aurangabad had reached Saswad. On March 29, Purandar was surrounded by Mughals. There was a fierce battle for 15 days.

On 14th April, the fort of Purandar was captured by the Mughals. Now the final battle had begun. Murarbaji Deshpande risked his life. He became immortal in Maratha history. Even today, if you ever go to Purandar, you can see the statue of Murarbaji and know the story of his bravery.

Before the treaty was signed, Shivaji Raje had sent a letter to Mirza Raja. This letter accurately describes the situation at that time and the state of mind of Shivrai.

Anticipating the current situation, Shivaji Raje decided to make a treaty with the Mughals. The treaty of Purandar took place.

Shivaji Raje lost all that they had earned in 16 years. The minimum strength to fight was left. Now,

He was accompanied by only his self-confidence, determination, Mother Jijau's blessings, and the dream of Swarajya. After this, Mirza Raja was feared that Shivaji would form a united front against the Mughals along with Qutub Shah and Adil Shah, so he informed Aurangzeb that Shivaji should be turned to him in any case. For that, I am sending Shivaji to your court.

Mirza Raja prepared Shivaji Raje for going to Agra and accordingly on 5th March 1666 Raje left for Agra. Aurangzeb himself had sent a letter to him on the occasion of his 50th birthday.

'Come and see me without any worries or doubts. You will be honored here and you will be allowed to return to the Deccan. 'Step by step, Shivaji Raje reached there with his 9-year-old son Shambhu Raje on 12th May.

Betrayal by Aurangzeb

If anyone has been found fearless in the fort of Agra, it was Shri Shivchhatrapati Maharaj. When the Mughal Empire was at the pinnacle of glory and power, and when Shivaji Raje was alone, publicly protested against the Aurangzeb. When Shivaji Raje returned to his homeland, did not imitate the Mughals, but built fortifications in various places for their resistance, for the freedom of the country.

After the incident took place in Agra fort, the result was decided. Shivaji Raje was taken to prison. The meaning was clear. Death.... when? How? Nothing was known. From the Deccan, Mirza Raja Jaisingh said,

'Don't kill Shivaji'.

If this has been done, then the situation will get out of hand here, sent a letter to Aurangzeb.

Aurangzeb decided to send Shivaji Raje on an expedition to Kabul. Of course, Shivaji Raje flatly refused to accept anything from the Aurangzeb. The situation was getting worse. Shivaji Raje knew that their death would come at any moment.

Plan of Escape from Agra

Finally, a plan was drawn up. It had become a thriller. Rumors were circulating in the Agra market about the king. Jaswant Singh himself was telling Aurangzeb that,

'Shivaji has divine power. He can jump 14-15 hands long. He walks 40-50 km in one shot.'

From the second day on, Aurangzeb increased the security around him. Sambhaji Raje, who was with Shivaji Raje, was not in captivity. They were allowed to walk. With him, Sarjerao Jedhe was extracting so much information about Agra.

The plan was slowly moving forward. On June 7, the king sent all his servants and army back to the Deccan.

Only Sambhaji Raje, Hiroji Farjand, Sarjerao Jedhe, Raghunath Ballal, Trimbak Sondev Dabir and Madari Mehtar were with him.

August 17, 1666, during the day, while 1000 soldiers were guarding, Shivaji Raje escaped from captivity. There is no such evidence as to how he escaped. There are some stories of 'Mithaicha Petara'. But it also was taken from Mughal documents.

Aurangzeb launched a search operation. But it was too late. A thrilling escape was a success. The kings crossed the last outpost of the Mughals on 20th August. Latif Khan was the watchman. When Aurangzeb found out about this, he exclaimed, Latif Khan, is an idiot.

Then in Agra, Raghunath Ballal Korde and Trimbak Sondev Dabir, the closest associates of Shivaji Maharaj, were found.

They were asked to unfold the mystery of Shivaji Raj's escape from Agra. But nothing was come out of the mouth. Had he spoken, Sambhaji Raje would have been especially captured from Mathura.

Shivaji Raje had taken a path beyond the reach of the Mughals without taking the road directly to the Deccan. From Mathura to Allahabad - Banaras - Gaya - Gondwana and from there to Rajgad. On the way, they came face to face with the enemy.

He showed himself as a Sage. Most traveled on feet. By hard work, the king reached to Deccan.

Rumours about death of Sambhaji Raje

Now leaving Sambhaji Raje to Vishwasrao in Mathura, Shivaji Raje hurried to the next path. What would they have felt leaving their 9-year-old son behind!!! But when it was dangerous to go together, they must have made that decision with a heavy heart. Sambhaji Raje was still in Mathura.

When Shivaji Raje reached Rajgad, everyone was very happy in swarajya. But Shivaji Raje didn't want to take any risk, so with a heavy heart; they spread rumors that his son sambhaji is no more.

Everyone was shocked by listening to this news. But it was a part of Ganimi kava (Guerrilla warfare). Aurangzeb realizes not to search for sambhaji now, he took back his army. When the road became safer, Vishwasrao took 9-year-old Sambhaji Raje and reached Rajgad himself.

Frustrated, Aurangzeb could not do much now. He thought, what should I do now? He had only one wave in his mind. A moment's carelessness has resulted in Shivaji's escape and a great price has to be paid for him in the future.

With the help of a 9-year-old Son, Chhatrapati Shivaji Raje managed to escape from the Agra. After the release of Shivaji Maharaj from captivity, they didn't want to take risk of Shambhu Raje's life and so they had to be kept in a safe place for some time.

Shivaji Maharaj kept him in Mathura for security reasons. Chhatrapati Shivaji Maharaj spread rumors of Shambhu Raje's demise to stop Mughals who were behind Yuvraj Sambhaji Raje. Shortly after he arrived in Maharashtra, Yuvraj Sambhaji Raje reached Swarajya safely.

Until the coronation of Chhatrapati Shivaji Maharaj in 1674, Shambhu Raje was well versed in politics and battle tactics. Due to his humble nature, he welcomed the delegates who came to Raigad for the coronation.

Matoshri Jijau died 12 days after the coronation of Chhatrapati Shivaji Maharaj. After that, there was no one left to pay attention to Shambhu Raje. Shivaji Maharaj was involved in the politics and battlefields of the Swarajya.

There is a very famous verse of the great Saint Jagatguru Tukaram Maharaj, which is quite relatable to Prince Shambhu Raje. That verse (Shlok) is given,

"पुत्र व्हावा ऐसा गुंडा !

ज्याचा तिन्ही लोकी झेंडा !!"

It means, the son should be such that his deeds should be great, his name should be known all over the world, He should be Good for the good people, the base of the helpless and bad for bad people. In all manners, this stanza was explaining the importance of Yuvraj Shambhu Raje.

Chhatrapati Shivaji Maharaj felt very proud of his son's ability and his love and affection towards the swarajya.

Father feels Proud

Chhatrapati Shivaji Maharaj was very proud to see the bravery of Shambhu Raje. Contemporaries used to call Sambhaji Sawai Shivaji.

Chhatrapati Shivaji Maharaj always used to say my 100 victories on one side and one victory of Shambhu Raje on one side. But his success was troubling to some people; the ministers had found it difficult to deal with Yuvraj Shambhu Raje. But Chhatrapati Shivaji Maharaj supported his son, which he knew Prince Sambhaji was the only one who can fight with anyone for Swarajya.

After the south Indian expedition, ministers start to hate Shambhu Raje & they didn't want Shambhu Raje as the next King due to Shambhu Raje's strictness.

In the Mahabharata, when the war was over, Arjuna asked Lord Krishna to come down. Arjuna was not aware about anything. When Lord Krishna stepped down from the chariot, the chariot broke and burns. Then Arjuna realizes that I survived only because of Lord Krishna, and Sambhaji believed that no one could defeat me as long as my father was with me.

Shivrai preaches to Sambhaji: Our enemies were different, your enemies are different. We knew our enemies, but you will not be able to recognize your enemies anytime soon.

Your enemies will attack you from behind. So always be careful. Take care of Swarajya, take care of family. If there is anyone in this world who can support us most, it is only the family.

"चारो दिशा मे पिता का था गुणगान, जिनके सामने हमेशा था वंदन,
उन्ही के पथ पे चलकर अमर हुआ शिवनंदन |"

Chapter III

GUERILLA WARFARE

In 1677, **Chhatrapati Shivaji Maharaj** had decided to capture south India. This news was spread everywhere. Aurangzeb who calls himself Badshah of Hindustan also got to know about this mission. He realized that this will be the best chance to destroy the Maratha kingdom because Shivaji will not be there. So he sent his one commander Diler Khan Pathan to attack on Maratha Swarajya.

Guerrilla tactics

Chhatrapati Shivaji Maharaj_was far ahead of thinking in terms of war tactics than any other king. He identified this gap & made a master plan. He knew that if there is any person who can fight with the Mughals in terms of Guerrilla warfare, he must be his son Prince Sambhaji Raje (Shambhu Raje). Prince Shambhu Raje was known for his political strategies. He was just 21 years old at that time.

The duo of father & son made one plan which was so unpredictable for the others. They made a scenario in which everyone was thinking that there is an internal conflict between Shivaji & Sambhaji. Everything is not good between father & son. Shambhu Raje was sent as Subhedar of Shringarpur by Chhatrapati Shivaji Maharaj & he moved to the south campaign.

Cavalry and army build in Shringarpur

After some days of spending at Shringarpur One day, Shambhu Raje and Kavi Kalash met. Prince Sambhaji Raje was thinking about increasing the number of warriors and cavalry in Swarajya. Finally, it was decided to build big Cavalry. For small children, they made a playground. For young people, they started games of wrestling and area for workouts daily.

It all happened in the end.

So many children began to gather. They Enjoy training with Prince Shambhu Raje. They started to build a cavalry and warrior force.

The decision was taken unanimously. From the ports of Cheul, Dabhol and Rajapur, they used to buy thick-bred, well-bred horses.

Shambhu Raje told everyone,

In the future, we will use to gather brave Marathas and build a new army of at least two thousand cavalries.

Sardar Vishwanath said, "Yuvraj, you had an army of five thousand in shringarpur, so Why all these things are needed?"

Shambhu Raje replied,

"Our new team will be very courageous. Let's build it with such passion that,

Wherever these horses will go in the future, from there they will be recognized as Maratha force of Swarajya"

Prince ordered to people,

Go as fast as you can and buy new horses.

The Shambhu Raje wanted people from the common Kunbi, Bara Balutedar, and 18 Pagad castes.

The cavalry began to take shape.

It is very difficult to climb the right edge of the Prachitgad fort. Still, they survived with strong horses. The horse used to get weakness while climbing the high ridge.

The horses now can move forward through burning, mud, or even fire.

Shambhu Raje was preparing to strengthen the horses. Many people used to gather from the surrounding villages to watch the gymnastics.

As the Shambhu Raje was thinking, the same thing happened to Shambhu Raje. One day Sardar Vishwanath came from Raigad with a letter and in a depressing voice

He said, "Yuvraj, Rahuji Somnath has given this letter. Yours sincerely a brief explanation is needed. How can you build a new army without prior permission? "

Shambhu Raje questioned,

Why not?

Kavi Kalash said, "Sardar Vishwanathji, Please send it to Raigad. In the Coronation ceremony of Chhatrapati Shivaji Maharaj, Shambhu Raje has been declared as Prince. According to religious tradition, Children have the same rights as an investor. It is in the interest of our king Chhatrapati Shivaji Maharaj. They can make any decision."

Sardar Vishwanath bowed down. They left.

Relief from Draught

Prince Shambhu Raje was crossing the town and suddenly two or three hundred poor farmers and a crowd of Koli People intercepted Prince's squad.

Surveillance teams told them to "go, go back, and go back." They pull them back.

But "Oh king,, wait a minute," a farmer said.

How can we get justice? Who will give us justice in the absence of our beloved king Chhatrapati Shivaji Maharaj?

Prince Shambhu Raje pulled the reins and pulled his horseback.

As soon as Prince stopped, the farmers ran ahead without making any noise.

The activists chanted, "My king, the government, save me."

Sambhaji Raje realized that something serious was happening. He quickly jumped down. Following Shambhu Raje, the Kalash was also down. Farmers gathered around both of them.

He shouted, "Tell me how to live? Look at these letters of taxes.

Shambhu Raje asked,

"Look at me." "Who gave this?"

"The letters are Came from Raigad." Two or three small farmers at once spoke.

Shambhu Raje gets confused and said

"Kaviraj look. There is something special about this scam. Something bad is happening behind us."

Shambhu Raje further added, "When the subhedari (Power) of this area was given to us by the Chhatrapati Shivaji Maharaj,

Then what would be the reason? How does it come from Raigad?

Kavi Kalash took the paper from the hands of the farmers.

Kavi Kalash started to read the tax letter in a smooth tone,

"For many years the taxes on-farm has been full, that's why this letter has been sent."

"But whose sign is there on the papers?"

Kalash said,

"Rahuji Somnath. It is clearly mentioned in this letter Rahuji Somnath signed on it with the orders of Minister Anaji Pant Datto.

There was a wave of fear among the farmers who were starving. Eight to ten people knelt at the feet of Prince Sambhaji Raje and Princess Yesubai.

They began to cry, "What can we do, my lord?

Look, we have nothing in our hands. There is nothing on the farms for the last six or seven years. Crops need the water and there is a shortage of water.

There is no dam on the field and there is no crop. Many people are annoyed

There was no need for other proofs considering the weak, lean bodies of these people.

However, Prince Sambhaji Raje called Thanedar aside.

I apologize for the inconvenience. " Prince Shambhu gave the verdict on the spot. Shambhu Raje said no need to pay any tax this year.

The farmers started dancing there with the joy.

After getting the blessings from poor farmers, Princej's squad started running towards Shringarpur.

At night, the Kavi Kalash told Shambhu Raje in a hushed voice,

"I have done my best in the morning. Apologies to the special envoy of Raigad, But Raje, you are a part of the action"

Shambhu Raje politely asked,

"Do you have any doubts about me?"

"It simply came to our notice then. But it is also against the government

Taxes will not be missed. That's it.... "

As soon as the farmers can pay taxes, it should go to the Raigad.

"KaviRaj, we are the subhedar of this region. In our rights, we can make this decision. Besides, we are the prince of the Hindu nation."

Letters from Dilerkhan

In just two days, Diler khan's envoy arrived in Shringarpur with a new flower and secretly filed letters. The Kavi Kalash presented it to the Shambhu Raje.

Shambhu Raje was annoyed and said,

"Did this old man go crazy, has he lost his mindset?"

His eyes began to line up in the letter.

"Rustam-e-Deccan Sambhaji Raje!

Please do come to our camp.

The Alamgir Mughal King Aurangzeb wants to use to conquer the whole country with his army.

Sorry for the inconvenience, we do not have the right to talk in and about your family.

But still, we knew the pain of your heart. The true love of your father is on Soyarabai and Rajaram. He is not loving you and also not taking any care of you. That's why your father sends you out of Raigad.

All ministers are not respecting you like Prince, they all are against you. Don't you think you should join our camp?

So instead of dying with a humiliated mind, go to Alamgir Aurangzeb.

Hold our two hands. Tomorrow, when the Mughal king came to Deccan, he will appreciate you

"Your future will be very bright."

After getting too many letters, Prince Shambhu Raje just kept a hold on Diler Khan. Because there was a fear that as Chhatrapati Shivaji Maharaj was not present at that time in Swarajya, it might possible that Diler khan will attack Swarajya by taking this advantage.

Meanwhile, Diler khan had come up with a huge army to finish the Maratha kingdom. Shambhu Raje was alone with a small number of soldiers. The Maratha soldiers were weary & tired after the south campaign, so to stop Diler Khan, one mind game was played by Shambhu Raje.

To execute the guerrilla tactics, Shambhu Raje played a trick on Diler Khan & sent him a letter explaining that I am not happy with my father. Diler khan was happy after listening to this. He again sent him a proposal to join the Mughal camp. There were lots of letter communications between them. Diler khan was very happy but he was not aware that he will be fooled.

Execution of Plan

In the Rainy season, at the banks of the Krishna River in Mahuli (near Satara) Shambhu Raje joined their camp by crossing the Krishna River. Shambhu Raje was aware that his life will be in danger. But for him, Chhatrapati Shivaji Maharaj was everything and the execution of the plan was much needed to avoid battle.

Aurangzeb was in shock & realized it was a trap. He sent a letter to Diler Khan & ordered to attack swarajya at any cost. Diler Khan had forced Shambhu Raje to either win the Bhupalgad or he will destroy its walls with bombs.

To save the lives of his fellow soldiers, Shambhu Raje wins that fort for Mughals without attacking. Some people were imprisoned; Khan ordered them to cut their hands. Shambhu Raje confronted Diler Khan & also save their life.

After this, in a very short time, Marathas recaptured that fort.

Now, Aurangzeb became very angry & got frustrated. He sent 5000 extra soldiers to arrest Shambhu Raje. Chhatrapati Shivaji Maharaj realized this situation & felt that his son's life is in danger. They Communicate with Shambhu Raje via spies to return to the nearest Maratha Fort Panhala.

While escaping, Shambhu Raje fought with Diler's advisor & commander Mulla Ahmed and cuts his hand. Chhatrapati Shivaji Maharaj sent his spies-cum-soldiers for this rescue operation.

Prince Shambhu Raje escaped safely from the Mughal camp & reached Panhala Fort. Chhatrapati Shivaji Maharaj himself came to meet his brave son

& it was known as one of the greatest historical meetings. Both father & Son met each other at Panhala fort.

They might have discussed the politics to be made in future as well as the family decisions. Every one was blaming Prince Sambhaji for joining the Mughal camp, but only one person was stand confidently with Prince Shambhu & that was Chhatrapati Shivaji Maharaj. They were very confident & proud of Prince Shambhu.

Due to some guerilla tactics, Mugahl Chieftain Diler khan was unable to attack on Swarajya in the absence of Chhatrapati Shivaji Mahraj. That's what both Shiv-Shambhu wanted to happen.

"बचपन मे भी गया था, वो जवानी मे भी गया था,
दुष्मन के तट पे वो बस स्वराज्य बचाने ही गया था |"

Chapter IV

SHREE SAKHI

There is no bravery without strength, there is no strength without courage, there is no courage without confidence, and likewise King Chhatrapati Sambhaji Maharaj was incomplete without Maharani Yesubai.

Marriage of King Sambhaji & Yesubai

Chhatrapati Shivaji Maharaj thought that Shambhu Raje should be married now. After consulting with Rajmata Jijau, Shambhu Raje married to (Rajau) Yesubai. Yesubai Shirke was the daughter of Sardar Pilajirao Shirke of Shringarpur.

At the time of marriage, one of the enemies tried to attack Shivaji Raje to get revenge. (Shivaji

Raje Attacked on Shaista Khan a few days ago) Shambhu Raje very bravely defends himself from attacker & enemy was captured by Marathas.

After getting married, Rajau came to Rajgad. Originally a clever and sensible Yesubai, she got the guidance from the Rajmata Jijau.

This aspect was vanished; the women of the Swarajya were not limited to a few children and grandchildren.

Abasaheb Chhatrapati Shivaji Raje did not let his daughter-in-law miss anything. Whether it is Ausaheb or Soyarabai, Putlabai, Sakwarbaisaheb, all the worldly things that we were not fortunate enough to share, were put in the place of our daughter-in-law.

Attorney General (Kulmukhtyar) Yesubai

Chhatrapati Sambhaji Maharaj told to Maharani Yesubai, this Swarajya was extended by my grandmother Rajmata Jijau and my father Chhatrapati Shivaraya.

We have to decide how to protect it. We want to protect this Swarajya in any situation. For that, you stand firm with me.

While everyone was wondering that who should be assigned the seal of Swarajya after Rajmata Jijau,

Chhatrapati Shivaji Maharaj gave this seal to Maharani Yesubai and gave her a big responsibility.

Mahrani Yesubai passed it properly.

Whenever Chhatrapati Sambhaji Maharaj went on a mission, Maharani Yesubai was taking the responsibility of Swarajya herself. No work could be done without her command.

The awakening of the society in which women were underestimated took place through this one thing. Chhatrapati Sambhaji Raje gave great respect to his wife and also taught her politics. This shows the intensity of Chatrapati Sambhaji Maharaj's thoughts.

After the loss of life of Chhatrapati Shivaji Maharaj, Aurangzeb came to Maharashtra with a military of lakhs of Mughals to interrupt the shackles of Swarajya.

It changed into his purpose that Swarajya could be effortlessly taken over after the departure of Chhatrapati Shivaji Maharaj. But Chhatrapati Sambhaji Maharaj thwarted Aurangzeb's plan.

With an army of enemies on one aspect, Siddhi on the alternative, Portuguese and Mughal on the opposite side, Chhatrapati Sambhaji Maharaj dusted off the enemy along with his may.

He was assisted on this with the aid of his lucky Maharani Yesubai. From the time of judgment, they had been taking care of Swarajya with that vigor.

Some congregations in the Swarajya have been already gnashing their teeth at Chhatrapati Sambhaji Maharaj.

Strong Support for Life

After the visit to Agra, when the news of Prince Sambhaji Raja's death was spread and yesubai realized what the world was like, she had to live as a widow for a few months. From this one incident, the young girl must have realized that her future life would be tough and responsible. Chhatrapati Sambhaji Maharaj had a great sadness in his mind that he was not on the south Indian expedition. His mind was very unstable.

While Prince Shambu Raje was in Shringarpur, Yesubai took care of Prince Sambhaji Maharaj's stormy mind. She made sure that they were not harmed in any way.

When Chhatrapati Sambhaji Maharaj was poisoned by own people, Yesubai stood firmly with him. She saw Swarajya properly as the Kulmukhtyar, so Chhatrapati Sambhaji Maharaj got strong support from her. Treasonous and treacherous people were punished, in which Maharani Yesubai played a key role.

She took care that no injustice would be done to anyone and assured that justice would be done in proper & defined manner. After the Maharani Soyarabai's departure, she took care of Rajaram Maharaj like his mother.

"पुरुषो की दुनिया मे जब औरत को कम समझा था,
तब उसी शंभु ने पत्नी को राजपाठ पढाया था |"

Chapter V

PRINCE SAMBHAJI: POET & WRITER

Battling in opposition to the large Mughal armed force with mental fortitude and excellent valiance, this successful Chhatrapati become additionally a superb author and an awesome expert of Sanskrit. Chhatrapati Sambhaji Maharaj composed 'Budhbhushan' in Sanskrit, while 'Naikabhed', 'Nakhshika' and 'Satsatak' in Braj.

As a teenager, he interacted with researchers like Kalash, Mahakavi Bhushan, and Gagabhatta and changed into suffering from the useful administration of his father Chhatrapati Shivaji Maharaj.

There are matters like responsibilities, bureau, and so forth Chhatrapati Sambhaji Raje introduced writing below the names of King Shambhu, Nripashambhu, and Shambhuvarman. His Sanskrit gift letter is well known, Satsatak in Braj language, Nakhshika, Nayakabheda is obtainable.

In the stunning weather of Shrungarpur, he composed the book 'Nakhshikha' with the incentive of Shri Sakhi Maharani Chhatrapati Yesubaisaheb. Prince Sambhaji Raje controlled the acquisition of Mumbai in English.

This second blessed Chhatrapati of the Swarajya changed into awareness of Marathi, Sanskrit, Persian, Urdu, Arabic, Braj, English, and numerous special dialects. Chhatrapati Sambhaji Maharaj turned into the expert of numerous sciences and expressions and turned into enriched with all temperances.

Budhbhushan

Budhbhushan carries verses on Sheshnag, Garuda, Jeebha, Bhramar, Kumbh, Pisces, Camel, Dundubhi, Neem tree, Gold, etc. Also, there are 7 verses related to the sun, 7 verses associated with the moon, three verses associated with air, 7 verses related to honey, 5 verses related to the elephant, 19 ve8rses related to various trees.

Budhbhushan is a Sanskrit textual content written through Chhatrapati Sambhaji Raje 350 years ago in the past. Chhatrapati Sambhaji Raje started out penning this book at the age of fourteen. He finished this book at the age of seventeen. It has 3 chapters.

The original manuscript carries 883 verses. Budh is the intellect, the ornament of the mind. Budhbhushan is a Sanskrit textual content written via Chhatrapati Sambhaji Maharaj. In this book, Shambhu Raje has mentioned how to run the administration, what should be the regulations.

In this book, Prince Sambhaji Raje has spoken approximately about the sharpness, erudition, and divine vision in politics. Shaktapantha has power over their thoughts. They mean the integrity of nature and manhood. Shiva and Shakti are one and equal. Shaktipatha is given significance in Shaktapantha. In this book, he has studied numerous religious streams and brainstormed religious ideologies.

Beautifully penned on Lord Ganesha

Chhatrapati Sambhaji Maharaj pays homage to Lord Ganesha by paying homage to Lord Shankar and Lord Parvati of Shivkula.

देवदानवकृतस्तुतिभागं हेलया विजितदर्पितनागम् ।
भक्तविघ्नहनने धृतरयलं तं नमामि भवबालकरलं नमामि ।

It is our historical culture to begin any auspicious deed by using paying homage to Lord Ganesha. Prince Sambhaji Maharaj has imitated his historical culture via praising Lord Ganesha at the very beginning of his book on politics, Budhbhushan.

In this book, Prince Sambhaji Maharaj has written a few greater verses worshiping Ganesha. Chhatrapati Shivaji Maharaj additionally performs the first worship of Shree Ganesha in any function.

This is not sudden.

Under the guidance of his mother, Shivaraya had begun the work of preserving his society and building Swarajya in Pune. Pune was ruined during the Sultanate duration by means of turning a donkey's plow, hitting an iron pass, and striking a small van on it. After this, Pune becomes dewy.

People have been afraid to settle in Pune.

The fear of the Sultan's restraint, the fear of wild beasts as well as the concern of turning the donkey's plow, crossing it, and placing a small van on it became additionally a surprise to the religious thoughts of that point. Therefore, it is dangerous to settle in Pune now. There became a fear within the minds of the villagers that human beings could no longer be capable of standing there again.

It was necessary to give you some spiritual answer. It should be stated that plowing the land with gold plow and establishing Kasba Ganpati was related to this.

Praised Gods in Budhbhushan

Prince Sambhaji Raje's erudition can be seen through searching at the political verses within the second chapter. He seems to have taken the basis of Kamandakiya Nitisara, Vishnudharmottarpurana, Matsya Purana, Mahabharata, Manu, and Yajnavalkya. He has paid homage to Lord Shivshankar, Parvati, Bhavani Devi, Lord Krishna, Lord Ganapati, Gautam Buddha, and Baliraja.

He has popularized the Buddha as a symbol of compassion. He had studied Jain, Buddhist, Lokayat, etc. Sects, it's miles felt at the same time as analyzing 'Budhbhushan'.

In this book, Prince Sambhaji Raje's vision is coordinated. In the primary verses, the deity Vandana is the suffix of their subtle remark, religious examine. In this, together with the deities, they have got also worshiped the Guru.

The description of the bravery of his grandfather Shahaji Raje and father Shivaji Raje is given in Swakul Varnan, he's a heroic hero. It expresses the real pride of our extended family.

'आपूर्वांचल पश्चिमाम्बुधिमथाप्यासेतु शीताचलं |
निर्जित्यावनिमण्डलं च करदीकृत्या खिलान्भूमिपान् ||
श्रौतं धर्ममव्याप सध्दिरुमभित!राजाभिषके परं :
छत्राद्यैर्नृपलक्षणैसुदिनं सिंहासन राजते ||'

This means that all the territories inside the east, from the western seas, as well as from the famous Ramsetu to Himachal Pradesh, conquered the kings of the earth and compelled them to pay taxes.

Accepted the People Dharma and coronated to the reality. Identically, due to Chhatrapati Shivaji Raje, the throne became beautiful. The people had been glad and survived.

While praising Bhavanimata, the beautiful idol is well described with ornaments. She has been praised for making the scripture easy. It indicates the faith in her description. He mentions that she is Shiva's spouse. Describing Shiva, Prince Sambhaji Maharaj writes-

शशांकमौली भसीतेनं भासुर पंचानन शैलसुताधिनाथम
त्र्यक्षम गिरीश दशबाहुमंडीत कुबेरमित्र सतत नमामि

Meaning: The one who have the moon on their head, the one who look white because of the ash on the body, the one who have five faces, who is the husband of Parvati, the daughter of the Himalayas, who have three eyes, who are lord of the lords, Dharmaveer Shreeshambhu Chhatrapati always pays homage

विरिंचीविष्णुवंदीतं नगाधिराजकन्यकाविभूषितार्धविग्रहं प्रभूतबंदिसंस्तुतम् ।
लसज्जटातटस्फुरत्सुरापगावि-निःसरद्विशुद्धवारिशीतलं नमामि चंद्रशेखरम् ।।

Meaning: Brahma and Vishnu also worship Lord Shiva. Half of Mahadev's body is adorned by the Himalayan girl mother Parvati. Many devotees chant such praises to Lord Shiva. As the pure water of this Ganga flows from their body, their body is cooled.

I (Sambhaji Maharaj) pay homage to Shiva (holding the moon).

Praising the Clan

भृशबदान्वयसिन्धू सुधाकरः प्रथितकीर्तिरूदारपराक्रमः |
अभवतर्थकलासु विशारदो जगति शाहनृपः क्षितिवासवः ||

Meaning: The all-powerful king of the earth, or the incarnation of the real Shiva, the generous mighty and the master of economics and politics, this Shahaji Raje were adorned like the moon in the ocean.

येनाकर्णविकृष्टकार्मूकचलत्काण्डावलीकीर्ति |
प्रत्यर्थिक्षितीपालमौलिनिवहैरभ्यर्चि विश्वंभरा||
यस्यानेक वसुंधरा परिवृढ प्रोत्तुंग चूडामणे: |
पुत्रत्त्वं समुपागत: शिव इति ख्यात पुराणो विभु: ||

Meaning: The noblest of the world was born as the son of Shahaji. King Shivaji, who looked like a mountain (Himalayan), the greatest man in the Puranas, like Shiva, became a great son of Shahaji Raje.

तस्यात्मज:शंभुरिति प्रसिध्द:समस्तसामन्त शिरोवतंस:|
य:काव्यसाहित्यपुराणगीतकोदण्डविद्याऽर्णव पारगामी||

Meaning: King Shambhu, who was adorned as a head ornament in all the temples of such great Lord Shiva. He was well versed in poetry, literature, music, archery etc.

Politics Chapter

The second chapter is the soul of this book. It is political. The king and the king's signs and symptoms are in it. Scholarly, knowledgeable approximately the troubles of the bad, gentlemanly, intelligent, affected person, amassing wealth, spending accurately, smart in speech, knowledgeable in coronary heart, secret counselor, being like father and mother to the people.

In this chapter, Prince Sambhaji Raje says that there need to be a king who is from a very good family, cultured, humble, efficient, virtuous, a collection of virtuous human beings, a long way-sighted, one that conquers anger, one who is prudent, one that behaves wisely, one who punishes wrongly, one who isn't always emotionless.

He has similarly defined Shivniti. By analyzing the enemy, whilst explaining the approach of the way to damage it, this approach explains when to apply the virtues of bond, possibility, evil, warfare. After that, the king's assistant, Rajyange has come. These include Swami, Amatya, Janpad, Durg, and Shasan. Kanmantra Raja has instructed people on the way to get paintings executed.

The king must be benevolent. There ought to be someone who chooses the right minister. The king needs to take a look at it whilst making the appointment. Wise people must be given the right location. Prince Sambhaji Raje says that whilst appointing the Prime Minister, Minister, Amatya, Secretary, one needs to evaluate the deserves.

Do & Don'ts of King

काले मृदुर्यो भवति काले भवति दारूण: ।
राजा लोकद्वयापेक्षी तस्य लोकद्वंय भवेत ॥

Meaning: The King should have soft & tough attitude. At any time, he should be able to change the mind according to the situation.

भृत्यैः सह महीपालः परिहासं च वर्जयेत् ।
भृत्याः परिभवन्तीह नृपे हर्षवशंगतम् ॥

Meaning: The king should not make jokes with the servant. If King is doing fun with his servants, it could be very dangerous to the kingdom.

तुरंगमाणां प्रतिकल्पिता
नामेकोगजः षष्टिशतानि हन्ति ।
तस्माद्यतो भूरिजलस्तु पन्था
यतोन्नपानोपचितो विशङ्कः ।।

Meaning: A well-trained elephant is capable of killing six hundred horses in battle. Therefore, the king should follow the path without any hesitation, by consuming food and drink in the way where abundant water is available.

तेनाभियायायाज्जनयन्प्रतापं
शनैः शनैश्श्रमयन्बलानि ।
न ह्युन्नतानामणिनप्युदारं
पश्चात्प्रकोपं जनयेदरीणाम् ।।

Meaning: While the king is following the same path (as stated in the above verses), he should continue to move forward slowly, showing his glory and giving the army the rest it needs. Even if an enemy king higher than you comes forward, you should show anger against him and carefully attack that enemy.

व्यसनानि च सर्वाणि भूपति: परिवर्जयेत् ।
सप्तदोषा सदा राज्ञा हातच्या व्यसनोदया: ॥

Meaning: Shambhu Raja mentioned seven faults as enemies of the king.

- Don't talk too much to anyone

- Do not speak harshly to anyone

- The king should not leave the kingdom without protection

- The king should not consume drugs, alcohol, marijuana

- Women should be treated with respect like mothers

- The king should not kill the poor, the wild and the domestic animals

- The King Should Stay Away From Gambling

Samaynay & Nayikabhed

Gagabhatta, a Brahmin Pandit, wrote a book in Sanskrit called Samayanaya, which he humbly offered & dedicated to Chhatrapati Sambhaji Maharaj. He was only 18 at the time.

Nayikabheda: This book is in Hindi Braj language. Chhatrapati Shivaji Raje took Yuvraj Sambhaji Raje everywhere since childhood. During the visit of Agra, he studied the Mughal court, Benaras, Mathura. In a few lines he describes the gopis of Mathura from the era of lord Krishna.

Extraordinary Vision

His huge vision is reflected inside the idea of the nation. The concept of a kingdom is born out of the king's virtues. The king has to contend with the storehouses. The book includes critical records about Durgadhyaksha, Jagprasasti, and Gajmahatta, types of elephants, deer, and energy. They tell the king's behavior and the king's responsibilities. The coverage of whilst the king ought to attack is also ironic.

This indicates the diffused study of conflict. From the precise descriptions of the usage of pressure, rebellion, guerrilla struggle techniques, and so on, it is clear how corrected Prince Sambhaji Raje's administration became.

Favorite verses from the Mahabharata are in the section 'Accepted Politics'. From that comes the suffix of their reading. These are all proverbs that can be useful for human lifestyles. Prince Sambhaji Raje's verses are useful to humans in real existence.

It accepts pundits and condemns fools. This shows the know-how and diplomacy of Sambhaji Raje. Many verses appear to condemn addicted, feminist guys. The chapter offers with 'scattered coverage'. These verses touch upon human nature, conduct, behavior.

He has given eight signs and symptoms of destruction. He says that such someone hates the clever, the discovered, the clever, and the maximum sincere human beings in the first place. Then he works against them. The book 'Budhbhushan' is a readable book even in today's democracy. Chhatrapati Shivaji Maharaj explained the edict. Similarly, Prince Shambhuraje wrote 'Budhbhushan'. This is the ethics of the way to be a leader with the person.

Apart from this, it's far book that nurtures the countrywide spirit. From this book, it's miles seen that the human personal and moral values of Prince Sambhaji Raje had been rewarding.

"एक कवी के जैसे उसका कोमल सा मन था,
लेकीन युद्धभूमी मे वही रुद्रसा तांडव करता था|"

Chapter VI

INTERNAL CONSPIRACY

The young Shambhu Raje often had disagreements with the experienced dignitaries of Chhatrapati Shivaji Maharaj's court. Yuvraj Sambhaji Raje was strongly opposed to the administration of Chhatrapati's Amatya Anaji Pant.

Chhatrapati Shivaji Maharaj often ignored Anaji Pant's mistakes as he was an experienced and efficient administrator. But it was difficult for Yuvraj Shambhu Raje to accept it. Anaji Dutto and other ministers went against Yuvraj Sambhaji Raje.

There were reports of Prince Sambhaji meddling in the expense assortment endeavors of these Ministers. Sambhaji regularly freely criticized those ministers whom he blamed for being oppressive and degenerate.

Some of the ministers began to treat Yuvraj Shambhu Raje with contempt; this was done only at the order of Anaji Pant.

Due to his opposition, he could not go on the expedition to South India with Chhatrapati Shivaji Maharaj. Also, in the absence of Shivaji Maharaj, the Ashta Pradhan Mandal refused to obey the orders of Yuvraj Sambhaji Raje.

Therefore, Chhatrapati Shivaji Maharaj had to send Prince Sambhaji Raje as Subhedar of Shringarpur in Konkan.

Conflict with Soyra Matoshri

Chhatrapati Shivaji Maharaj, who killed Afzal Khan and cut the fingers of Shaista Khan, who was brave, was unfortunately left helpless in Personal life.

The feeling that he had been deliberately kept away from the South Indian campaign remained in Shambhu Raje's mind.

As Subhedar of Shringarpur, Yuvraj Shambhu Raje decided not to collect taxes from the stricken people for one year.

Maharani Soyrabai and the ministers started propagating that Sambhaji Raje was an irresponsible administrator and not fit to rule the kingdom.

It is asserted that Sambhaji consistently had a disturbed relationship with his stepmother, Soyrabai.

She held a desire for her child, Rajaram. Soyarabai expected that Chhatrapati Shivaji Maharaj would announce the name of Rajaram as the (Prince) Yuvraj of the kingdom.

The bond between Shambhu Raje & Rajaram Raje

Strangely in a couple of letters, Prince Sambhaji has referenced his stepmother Soyrabai as being benevolent and adoring. Every time Shambhu Raje took his little step-brother with him.

He treated Rajaram with love & care. There were no conflicts between the brothers, but ministers wanted to disturb their relationship by changing the mind of Soyra Matoshri.

Rajaram was to be married in 1680. But since Prince Sambhaji's disharmony with Soyrabai, Sambhaji was not welcome to his own stepbrother's wedding.

Planning to arrest Shambhu Raje

At that point, Chhatrapati Shivaji Maharaj's unfavorable demise (on 3 April 1680) occurred in Fort Raigad. Huge numbers of Ministers, for example, Pralhad Niraji, Annaji Datto, Moropant

Pingale, Balaji Avaji Chitnis, Hiroji Farzand, and so forth, wanted Rajaram Raje as the next Chhatrapati.

With the help of Soyrabai, they introduced the ten-year-old Rajaram as the following Chhatrapati. Balaji Avaji even dispatched a letter routed to the killedar (the fortress authority) of Panhala to capture Yuvraj Sambhaji.

Janardhan Pant Hanumante was approached to arrest Sambhaji. Yet, the message was found by Prince Sambhaji's well-wishers, who quickly inform Shambhu Raje regarding the trick. Sambhaji and his men quickly assumed responsibility for the fortification.

The killedar was executed. 200 of the scammers were captured and executed.

Hiroji Farzand had figured out how to escape, however, was re-captured at Chiplun. Janardhan Pant Hanumante was also seized in Kolhapur.

Anaji Pant conspired with Soyra Matoshri for selecting the 10-year-old Son Rajaram Raje as the new Chhatrapati of Swarajya.

They started the preparation of the Coronation of Rajaram Raje with a few supporters & marched towards Fort Panhala to capture Shambhu Raje.

Sarsenapati Hambirrao Mohite

Prince Sambhaji Raje made sure about the help of some Maratha aristocrats, for example, Sarsenapati Hambirrao Mohite. The sarnobat (president) of the Maratha armed force, who was Soyrabai's brother and the father-in-law of Rajaram Raje.

Rajaram's better half, Tarabai, was his little girl. In any case, he favored Prince Sambhaji, whom he thought about as the legitimate beneficiary to the seat.

When Anaji Pant & other ministers reached fort Panhala to arrest Shambhu Raje, Sarsenapati Hambirrao Mohite stands with Shambhu Raje. Sarsenapati knew that if there is anyone who can fight with Aurangzeb, then it is only Shambhu Raje.

Sarsenapati refused to arrest Prince & wanted to punish all the ministers. Shambhu Raje asked Sarsenapati to capture these ministers.

Yuvraj Sambhaji Raje walked alongside 20,000 soldiers to Fort Raigad. Yesaji Kank, an old Chhatrapati Shivaji Maharaj's follower, opened the stronghold entryways for the sovereign.

Soyra Matoshri wanted to stop Shambhu Raje from entering the Raigad. Malsawant tried to oppose

Shambhu Raje at the bottom of the fort. Shambhu Raje defeated Malsawant at Pachad & arrested him. They gave death punishment to Malsawant.

Releasing all Conspirators

On 16 January 1681, Prince Sambhaji Raje was declared the new Chhatrapati (king) of the Maratha Empire. Samarth Ramdas did give Shambhu Raje a personal letter along with his blessings.

In the letter, Ramdas Swami advised the young king to follow in the footsteps of his great father, be more tolerant towards his people, and avoid making decisions in anger and haste and he advised Prince Sambhaji to be more discreet and prudent in the future.

अखंड सावधान असावे| दुश्चित कदापि नसावे|
तजविजा करीत बसावे| एकांत स्थळी||१||

काही उग्रस्थिती सांडावी| काही सौम्यता धरावी|
चिंता लागावी परावी अंतर्यामी||२||

मागील अपराध क्षमावे| कारभारी हाती धरावे|
सुखी करुनि सोडावे| कामाकडे||३||

पाटवणी तुंब निघेना| तरी मग पाणी चालेना|
तैसे सज्जनांच्या मना| कळले पाहिजे||४||

जनांचा प्रवाहों चालिला| म्हणजे कार्यभाग आटोपला|
जन ठायी ठायी तुंबला| म्हणिजे खोटे||५||

श्रेष्ठी जे जे मेळविले| त्यासाठी भांडत बैसले|
मग जाणावे फावले| गनिमासी||६||

ऐसे सहसा करू नये| दोघे भांडता तिसऱ्यासी जाए|
धीर धरून महत्कार्य| समजून करावे||७||

आधीच पडला धस्ती| म्हणजे कार्यभाग होय नास्ती|
याकारणे समस्ती| बुद्धि शोधावी||८||

राजी राखता जग| मग कार्यभागाची लगबग|
ऐसे जाणोनिया सांग | समाधान राखावे||९||

सकळ लोक एक करावे| गनीम निपटुन काढावे|
ऐसे करीता कीर्ति धावे| दिगंतरी||१०||

आधी गाजवावे तडाके| मग भूमंडळ धाके|
ऐसे न होता धक्के| राज्यास होती||११||

समय प्रसंग वोळखावा| राग निपटुन काढावा|
आला तरी कळो नेदावा| जनांमध्ये||१२||

राज्यामध्ये सकळ लोक| सलगी देवून करावे सेवक|
लोकांचे मनामध्ये धाक| उपजोचि नये||१३||

बहुत लोक मेळवावे| एक विचारे भरावे|
कष्टे करोनी घसरावे| म्लेंच्छांवरी||१४||

आहे तितुके जतन करावे| पुढे आणिक मेळवावे|
महाराष्ट्र राज्य करावे |जिकडे तिकडे||१५||

लोकी हिम्मत धरावी| शर्तींची तरवार करावी|
चढ़ती वाढती पदवी| पावाल येणे||१६||

शिवरायास आठवावे| जीवित्व तृणवत मानावे|
इहलोकी परलोकी राहावे| कीर्तिरुपे||१७||

शिवरायांचे आठवावे स्वरूप| शिवरायांचा आठवावा साक्षेप|
शिवरायांचा आठवावा प्रताप| भुमंडळी||१८||

शिवरायांचे कैसे चालणे| शिवरायांचे कैसे बोलणे|
शिवरायांची सलगी देणे| कैसे असे||१९||

सकळ सुखांचा त्याग| करुनी साधिजे तो योग|
राज्यसाधनाची लगबग| ऐसी असे||२०||

त्याहुनी करावे विशेष| तरीच म्हणावे पुरूष|
या उपरी आता विशेष| काय लिहावे||२१||

Chhatrapati Sambhaji Raje decided to forgive all
ministers. He released several of the conspirators. He

even reappointed Moropant Pingale as his Peshwa & Anaji Pant as Mujumdar.

The loyal Hambirrao Mohite was already commander-in-chief of the armed forces.

Akbar seeking help from King Shambhu

Aurangzeb's strict and political strategies were questionable to the point that a significant number of the cross classes who changed over to the Mughals had various perspectives on the framework, yet didn't dare to challenge the state.

Akbar was in the correct state of mind to oppose the lord. At the point when Akbar considered such insubordination to the framework, he needed to change the political uprising.

He felt that Chhatrapati Sambhaji Maharaj was the lone individual in front of him since he had the option to all the more likely comprehend his pain and responses.

The Mughal Badshah always used to say that his biggest enemy was King Sambhaji. The entire cycle was appropriately slowed down and the two youthful sovereigns shaped collusion. One was the top of the Maratha realm and the difference was the beneficiary of the Mughal realm. Holding hands, they were considering holding the edge. This prompted a quick activity and prompt usage.

King Sambhaji's strategy was answerable for supporting the Mughal cost; however, Chhatrapati Sambhaji Maharaj was careful and content in this exchange. He was genuinely thinking about raising the cost of the tycoon.

He believed that if this defiance fizzled, issues would emerge. The certified idea of the offer was additionally a genuine issue. So King Sambhaji needed to set aside some effort to arrive at the correct choice in a brief timeframe.

This inquiry regularly strikes a chord with regards to why King Sambhaji invested such a lot of energy to settle on the correct choice during this coalition.

He was anxious to concentrate on all the potential outcomes of the collision. Around then, he was settling on a troublesome issue for Prince Akbar. Political Friendship with Akbar was a significant piece of King Sambhaji's set of experiences.

On May 9, 1681, Akbar crossed the Narmada River and wanted to meet Shambhu Raje with his consultant Durgadas Rathod. Akbar stayed outdoors at Pali in Konkan.

Chhatrapati Sambhaji Maharaj and Akbar met at Pali on 1 November 1681 and intended to attack the north under the initiative of Durgadas Rathore. He felt that the Rajputs would rebel against the Mughals and with the assistance of Rajput Akbar a benevolent would be set up and the Rajputs would manage for his sake.

This excellent plan was ideal however needed a viable reality. In numerous outskirts of Maharashtra, the Mughal armed force had bombed wretchedly and King Sambhaji needed to take advantage of this lucky break to catch the Aurangzeb.

The Akbar was an insubordinate sovereign and he was not content with his father's arrangements.

He went to the Deccan to look for the help of the leaders of the south against his Father. The representative help given by Chhatrapati Sambhaji Maharaj was important. Chhatrapati Sambhaji Maharaj was making one stride after another mindfully. His procedure was to restrict misfortunes. If King Sambhaji had settled on a hurried choice, it would have been risky and hard for him.

Chhatrapati Sambhaji Maharaj felt that this was not the opportune chance to respond against the Mughal rule. So he followed the rule of keeping a watch out. Being cautious and the patient was the correct methodology to stay away from the different difficulties of King Sambhaji.

In this way, the terrific union with Akbar was a chance and an issue. Chhatrapati Sambhaji Maharaj confronted this cautiously and mindfully.

Again Conspiracy & End of Ministers

Anaji Pant wanted the upper position of the empire, he again started to conspiracy. The discredited ministers once again decided to take their chances by enlisting the help of the Mughal prince Akbar in overthrowing Chhatrapati Sambhaji Maharaj.

They tried to take Akbar over to their side and even Anaji Pant tried to kill Shambhu Raje by giving poison in the meal.

Anaji Datto & other colleagues approached Akbar with a proposal. The proposal was, Anaji will give all rights to Akbar & will announce Akbar as the new Badshah of Deccan in exchange for making Rajaram Raje the King of Swarajya. But Mughal Prince Akbar, grateful for the protection he had received, informed Chhatrapati Sambhaji Raje about the attempt to be made on his life. On hearing this news, Shambhu Raje decided to punish this selfish minister.

He arrested the conspirators (Anaji Datto, Somaji Datto, Hiroji Farzand, Balaji Avji, etc) and had them trampled under the feet of an elephant. Khando Ballal, the son of Balaji Avji joined Shambhu Raje as he felt that his father was on the wrong side.

After punishing the all Conspirators, Shambhu Raje started their new expeditions. They give honor to Sarsenapati Hambirrao Mohite for their loyalty. That's how Anaji pant & his colleagues were punished by Chhatrapati Sambhaji Maharaj for their crimes.

"शील जानने वाला वो शिलवंत, संस्कृतपंडित वो बुद्धिवंत,
एक भी लढाई हारने न वाला वो शौर्यवंत | "

Chapter VII

16 JANUARY 1681

The practice of following the footsteps of the father and entering into the same field is natural in the world. Often the son's deeds are overshadowed by the father's deeds, but in the case of Prince Sambhaji Raje, it is an exception.

Chhatrapati

The post of Chhatrapati, created by Chhatrapati Shivaji Maharaj, gave stability to the local people in the true sense. The belief that our kingdom, our system in which we can get all kinds of justice, security, and welfare under the shadow of an anointed king, was created in the minds of the people by the post of Chhatrapati.

It not only remained a position but became the basis of people's survival. It was a symbol of the implementation of the public welfare system over the oppressive system.

Coronation of Chhatrapati Sambhaji Maharaj

If a king dies, the question arises as to who will take his place. This was not the case even after the death of Chhatrapati Shivaji Maharaj. But disputes are deliberately created.

On 3rd April 1680, Chhatrapati Shivaji Maharaj died suddenly at Raigad. In the absence of Prince Shambhu Raje, some selfish court ministers tried to take the reins of power by placing Rajaram Raje on the throne. But they failed. Prince Shambhu Raje handled this difficult situation from fort Panhala and tried to fix the governance. But Swarajya needed another Chhatrapati.

The untimely departure of Chhatrapati Shivaji Maharaj gives big damage to Swarajya. Chhatrapati Shivaji Maharaj was the true king of the people. There was fear of a tyrannical system came to the minds of the people. However, Prince Shambhu Raje was crowned on 16th January 1681. He assured that the system of the time of Chhatrapati Shivaji Maharaj would continue.

Prime Committee

Chhatrapati Sambhaji Maharaj was also very good at governance. They were skilled organizer. As Chhatrapati Shivaji Maharaj, after becoming Chhatrapati, Sambhaji Maharaj had also appointed Ashta Pradhan Mandal. Nilopant Pingale as Prime Minister, Balaji Avji as Secretary, Hambirrao Mohite as Commander, Pralhad Niraji as Judge, Janardan Pant as Pant Sumant, Moreshwar Panditrao as Charity President, Abaji Sondev as Pant Secretary, Dattaji Pant as Pant Amatya, Annaji Dutto as Mujumdar Were appointed.

At the coronation on 16th January 1681, Chhatrapati Sambhaji Maharaj gave the title of 'Kulmukhtyar' to Maharani Yesubai. Kulmukhtyar is the person who runs the Swarajya in the absence of Chhatrapati.

She was included in the cabinet, but she also had the power to adjudicate. At the same time, a seal of his name was given as **'श्री सखी राज्ञी जयती'**.

Maharani Yesubai was the second woman from the Chhatrapati dynasty to have such rights after Rajmata Jijau.

The cabinet of King Sambhaji is given as follows,

Shrimant Chhatrapati Sambhaji Raje Shivaji Raje Bhosale (Commander-in-Chief of Senadhish-Supreme Authority)

Chhatrapati Yesubai Sambhaji Raje Bhosale (In charge of the monarchy in the absence of Sambhaji Raje)

Commander-in-Chief - Hambirrao Mohite

Prime head - Kavi Kalash

Peshwa - Nilo Moreshwar Pingale

Chief Justice - Pralhad Niraji

Charity President - Moreshwar Panditrao

Secretary - Balaji Avji

Surnis - Abaji Sondev

Dabir - Janardhan Pant

Mujumdar - Annaji Dutto

Wakenavis - Dattaji pant

Royal seal of Chhatrapati Sambhaji Maharaj

श्री शंभो: शिवजातस्य मुद्रा द्यौरिव राजते |

यदंकसेविनी लेखा वर्तते कस्य नोपरि ||

Like Chhatrapati Shivaji Maharaj, Prince Shambhu Raje also struck coins in his name on the occasion of his coronation.

The letter "Shri Raja Shambhu Chhatrapati" is engraved on the front of the coin and the letter "Chhatrapati" is engraved on the back.

16 January Celebrated Every Year

340 years ago, Chhatrapati Sambhaji Maharaj became the second Chhatrapati of the Maratha Empire. Still, people celebrate this occasion every year at Fort Raigad. This was a big occasion in the history of India. 16 January 1681 has special importance in the Maratha Empire.

After that day, Chhatrapati Sambhaji Maharaj fought with Aurangzeb, Portuguese, Sidhhi's, Britishers & other enemies. Precious protection was given by Chhatrapati Sambhaji Maharaj to the Maratha Empire in their 9 Years career in Politics.

That's why every year this day is celebrated as the Coronation of Chhatrapati Sambhaji Maharaj everywhere.

Chapter VIII

ATTACK ON MUGHAL EMPIRE

The Mughal Emperor Aurangzeb had finished his mission at Rajputana and was getting ready to attack on the Deccan with full power. Chhatrapati Sambhaji Maharaj realized that the Maratha Empire was in a consistent battle against a huge Mughal Empire. Prior to the appearance of Aurangzeb in the Deccan, the Maratha depository was to be filled.

After the passing of Chhatrapati Shivaji Maharaj, the Mughal ruler Aurangzeb marched towards Deccan and wanted to clear out the Maratha from

Deccan, their strategies most likely prompted the conclusion of the Mughals' goals with the Marathas.

Chhatrapati Sambhaji Maharaj was almost prepared to rebel against the Mughal attacks taking into account the potential barbarities submitted by Aurangzeb Badshah.

Chhatrapati Sambhaji Maharaj had tested the Mughal ability to eliminate deterrents and blocks in the Maratha realm of the Hindavi Swarajya.

Unlike his father, the circumstance in Shambhuraje's vocation was troublesome as there were Portuguese, English and Siddhis other than the Mughals.

Chhatrapati Sambhaji Maharaj tested the Mughals dependent on their voice and solid maritime base.

After Chhatrapati Shivaji Maharaj's passing, the Mughal ruler Aurangzeb felt that this was the correct opportunity to crush the opportunity cherishing Marathas.

The Maratha people group was separated and there was a gathering of some of the representatives against Chhatrapati Sambhaji Maharaj.

Aurangzeb needed to exploit the present circumstance and he had arranged a mission against the Marathas. He knew and aware of everything that Chhatrapati Sambhaji Maharah might do.

Chhatrapati Sambhaji Maharaj likewise needed to get a psychological triumph over his adversary Aurangzeb by getting the main triumph.

Plan to loot Burhanpur

After the crowning celebration of Chhatrapati Sambhaji Maharaj, he gathered an essential gathering of his consultants and senior officers at Raigad.

Chhatrapati Sambhaji Maharaj and the Maratha officers chose to assault and loot Burhanpur as it was a significant exchanging focus and an exceptionally prosperous city.

This city was much closed to the heart of Aurangzeb. The separation from Raigad to Burhanpur was in excess of 500 km. A multitude of 8,000 protected the city.

Chhatrapati Sambhaji Maharaj had gotten the news that Subhedar Bahadur Khan of Burhanpur was going to Aurangabad for his nephew's wedding with a little girl of the princess of Abul Hasan Qutb Shah's administration.

Bahadur Khan took power 3000 with him for marriage. Accordingly, under the authority of Kakar

Khan, the deputy of Bahadur Khan, Burhanpur had 5,000 soldiers left.

Prior, Chhatrapati Sambhaji Maharaj and his commanders constrained the front at Burhanpur to assault Surat and chose to partition it into two additional parts.

At Burhanpur, the Mughals had to re-visitation of Surat. Chhatrapati Shivaji Maharaj had taken out them twice previously.

Maratha attacked on Mughals

Sarsenapati Hambirrao Mohite arrived at the timberland close to Burhanpur with an army of 15000 in number rangers.

Kakar Khan revitalized the non military personnel armed force and chose to assault Hambirrao at 12 PM. At the point when he emerged from the city doors, Chhatrapati Sambhaj Maharji himself assaulted the old quarry with a multitude of 4,000 cavalry.

Chhatrapati Sambhaji Maharaj's military moved the station of the ill-equipped Mughal armed force.

Chhatrapati Sambhaji Maharaj then left 300 troopers at the entryways of the fundamental city and went to Bahadurpura, the most extravagant suburb of the city. Discussions started to burglarize the homes of well off dealers appeared to him by his covert agents.

Sarsenapati Hambirrao's military before long joined Chhatrapati Sambhaji Maharaj and the consolidated Maratha powers began plundering the city.

From that point onward, Sarsenapati Hambirrao Mohite fixed the doors of the city so the message of the assault would not spread. The Marathas plundered for three days straight.

The Marathas plundered about Rs 2 crore. The Marathas caught the fortress of the city and captured Kakar Khan.

Bahadur Khan heard the news and promptly left Aurangabad with an enormous armed force to save Burhanpur.

At the point when the Marathas heard this, they quickly fled the city as they were far away from the Maratha outskirts.

Kakar Khan & Jijia

Mughal chieftain Kakar Khan had tried to impose a tax called Jijia in the Swarajya. He blocked Saint Tukaram Maharaj's palanquin and started harassing the Warakari people.

This was in Chhatrapati Sambhaji Maharaj's mind since then. He caught Kakar Khan and taught him a good lesson. Kakar Khan tried to attack on Chhatrapati Sambhaji Maharaj, but he did not succeed.

Chhatrapati Sambhaji Maharaj killed him and freed the people from Jijia tax.

Earlier, Bahadur Khan also attacked on palanquin near Pedgaon; however King Shambhu provided protection to them at that time also. Swarajya's army was given to the Warakari people for the protection of the palanquin. Every year since then, Chhatrapati Sambhaji Maharaj has protected Lord Vitthal's Wari from the Invaders.

Coming back to Raigad with Loot

Chhatrapati Sambhaji Maharaj left Burhanpur and began walking towards Raigad. Bahadur Khan caught a multitude of around 20,000 from Aurangabad to reimburse the loot from the Marathas.

Now, Chhatrapati Sambhaji Maharaj separated his military into three sections. He realized the situation very quickly.

There were two roads to Raigad, short through Dharangaon-Chopda and long by means of Erandol.

On the principal course, Bahadur Khan was sitting tight for Chhatrapati Sambhaji's soldiers.

The represetatives of the primary division of Chhatrapati Sambhaji Maharaj under Mulla Qazi Haider took this way. Bahadur Khan captured all these yet he was persuaded that Chhatrapati Sambhaji Maharaj would go far to keep away from his military.

Some time later, another division of the Maratha armed force, comprising of 3000 troopers, followed a similar course with no plundering.

Bahadur Khan didn't assault them regarding the plundering. Subsequent to seeing this force, Bahadur Khan was persuaded that Chhatrapati Sambhaji Maharaj had picked far and left for Erandol.

Three hours after Bahadur Khan left the primary course, the remainder of the Maratha armed force plundered on a similar Dharnegaon-Chopda course to arrive at the Maratha stronghold of Salher. Also, in a brief timeframe the Marathas arrived at Raigad.

Bahadur Khan, in the interim, had left Aurangabad in an enormous power with a couple of troops left. Seeing this chance, a Maratha Sardar named Suryaji Kakde assaulted Aurangabad with a multitude of 7,000 through Paithan.

Bahadur Khan promptly arrived at Aurangabad by means of Fardapur and Suryaji Kakde needed to pull out from the city.

Counter attack on Pathans

Aurangzeb had raised some significant rangers Ahadi Pathans in each significant Mughal city. Their work was to discover the head of the foe armed force in the event of an assault.

At the point when Chhatrapati Sambhaji Maharaj left Burhanpur for Raigad, five Pathans from Burhanpur began pursuing the returning Maratha armed force.

Chhatrapati Sambhaji Maharaj went to Vani with a little armed force to go to Saptashrungi sanctuary and was assaulted; however he got away in fight.

To capture Chhatrapati Sambhaji Maharaj, the Aurangzeb Badshah took pictures of Chhatrapati Sambhaji Maharaj from ministers all over the state and sent them to Pathans. Day and night Pathans were searching for Chhatrapati Sambhaji Maharaj but they could not find anything except despair.

On his way to Raigad, Chhatrapati Sambhaji Maharaj slowly sent troops in different directions. Chhatrapati Sambhaji Maharaj himself stayed in a village for a few days, but in the end some villagers betrayed him by seeing the picture that Pathan had shown to them.

Pathans got a hint of Chhatrapati Sambhaji Maharaj; they reached at night and attacked Chhtrapati Sambhaji.

The brave Chhtrapati Sambhaji confronted them, forced them to withdraw from the war and said with a thud, go and show this picture to your emperor.

"Even if Shiva is gone, Rudra is still left." Again, if you go against us, we will dig your grave here in Maharashtra.

Seige of Ramshej Fort

Aurangzeb's army consisted of extra than 5 million infantrymen and his navy base gave the impression of a small city.

So, Aurangzeb believed that this would be a small undertaking and so he decided to start his campaign by way of attacking the sort of big fortress known as Ramshej. After all, his father Shah Jahan had additionally commenced the Deccan campaign by way of attacking Ramshej Fort.

The Mughals commenced their campaign by way of attacking Ramshej in April 1682. Shahabuddin Khan, together with Hayat Khan and

Dalpat Rao, besieged it. They numbered within the heaps.

Meanwhile, some Maratha squaddies had been guarding the fortress. Moreover, the Mughal army had introduced massive and heavy guns and different devices of the imperial navy. But a small detachment of Marathas defended the citadel with none breach.

In truth, consistent with Kafi Khan's contemporary file, the Marathas did now not have cannons on the fortress. Instead, they made guns out of timber and used cannonballs made from animal arrows.

At the same time, Chhatrapati Sambhaji Maharaj became not unaware of the continued conflict. Sarsenapati Hambirrao Mohite himself led an army to attack the Mughals and divert their interest from the siege.

Rupaji Bhosale and Manaji More additionally attacked Shahabuddin Khan's army in a close-by village of Ramshej.

Four months after the siege ended, Chhatrapati Shivaji Maharaj and his son Chhatrapati Sambhaj Maharaji had a policy of keeping sufficient ammunition even on the forts having no cannons or weapons.

Ramshej became no exception to that and even though it did no longer have cannons it had sufficient ammunition. The citadel commander had an idea and utilized amply to be had animal pores and skin and wooden on the fort to make wood cannons.

Bahadur Khan Kokaltash turned into distraught and found that Marathas have been receiving secret elements from the nearby forts. He carefully blocked all the paths to close by Maratha forts. There became a dire shortage of food in the fortress.

Seeing this case, Maratha King Sambhaji Raje acted quickly employing sending his sardars Rupaji Bhosale and Manaji More with the army and supplies.

The forces clashed at Ganeshgaon. They attempted to break the Mughal line but had been not able to deliver the fortress. Rupaji Bhosale was wounded in the battle.

Chhatrapati Sambhaji Maharaj became in great worry that his fiercely brave warriors have been fighting without meals.

One day, because of the excessive awful climate Bahadur Khan Kokaltash relaxed his encirclement for sooner or later enabling Rupaji Bhosale and Manaji More to deliver the fortress with substances sufficient for six greater months. Bahadur Khan then attempted to win the fort with the assist of a ' exorcist' as he believed that the Marathas had ghosts under their control.

The Marathas once more fooled him because the exorcist changed into himself a Maratha soldier in cover who led the Mughal Army in a lethal ambush of the Marathas.

Bahadur Khan Kokaltash and Mughals fled the lethal ambush and several Mughals have been killed in this wonder attack.

Aurangzeb threw his crown

Aurangzeb learned a thing from Ramshej's siege. If it takes so long to get a fort, when will I get 350+ forts of Chhatrapati Shivaji Maharaj? If this continued, he would have known that even after seven generations, Swarajya would not be in his hands.

No matter what, it is impossible to defeat Chhatrapati Sambhaji Maharaj. Aurangzeb felt very humiliated due to the Chhatrapati Sambhaji

Maharaj's attack on Burhanpur. He did not tolerate the attack.

He said, I thought that Chhatrapati Shivaji Maharaj was no more, so I remained unaware, but his son turned out to be ten times dangerous than his father.

"I will not put this crown on my head till I catch this Sambha (Chhatrapati Sambhaji Maharaj)", so he threw away the crown. He made such a vow.

Emperor Aurangzeb, who had such a large empire from Kabul to Bengal, was defeated by King Sambhaji Maharaj.

He started thinking about the only thing that How to capture Chhatrapati Sambhaji and where? He knew that it was impossible to defeat Chhatrapati Sambhaji Maharaj in the war.

But the moment he threw the crown it was Chhatrapati Sambhaji Maharaj's big victory.

Chapter IX

SIDDHI & JANJIRA

The Janjira Fort was in the possession of the Negro Siddhi brothers. Janjira was a very important fort in the Arabian Sea and there was a barrage of guns on all sides.

It was also a financially important place because the sailors could keep an eye on the people and the merchants had to pay a large amount to get through the fort. The Marathas tried to win Janjira many times in the past but failed.

At that time Siddhi Khairiyat Khan and Siddhi Kasam Khan were on Janjira. These were Negroes from Africa. These Negroes were come out of the Janjira fort & caught the men on the shore, cutting off their ears and noses.

To take care of the women of Konkan, People suffering from this came to Shambhu Raje, they told their crisis to the king. Hearing all these horrible things, Chhatrapati Sambhaji Raje became very angry.

They decided to attack Janjira. But they knew that Janjira was difficult to win in a straight fight because the sea was there to help Janjira. So Shambhu Raje decided to go with guerrilla tactics.

Kondaji Farzand enters in Janjira

Shambhu Raje called Kondaji Farzand for the same. Who was Kondaji Farzand? He was the person who captured the Panhala fort with only 60 mavlas in the night for Swarajya.

Shambhu Raje told his plan to Kondaji and then Kondaji left. He took 40-50 Maratha's with him and left. And came directly to Janjira's Siddhi, and told Siddhi that he wished to accept his job.

Siddhi was shocked. He was delighted. Because a brave Maratha of Shambhu Raje had come to them. Siddhi gave him his job.

And then what, Kondaji started serving Siddhi. But Siddhi was not aware of the plan of Kondaji. In swarajya also, people thought that kondaji was not happy with the decisions of Shambhu Raje & that's why he went to siddhis of Janjira.

Shambhu Raje & Kondaji pretends that they are enemies of each other & that's why Sidhhi Khairiyat Khan trust Kondaji & kept him in Janjira fort.

Chhatrapati Sambhaji Maharaj's plan to Kondaji was to blow up all the Ammunition Storage of Janjira. And for this daring move, he had sent Kondaji and a select few Maratha in Janjira. Almost after months, kondaji & his colleagues were settled in Janjira & they came to know about each place on Janjira.

Kondaji saw the Ammunition storage & decided to blast it. But without consulting with Shambhu Raje, it was very risky so he stops himself for the day. He communicates with Shambhu Raje via spies & in hidden mysterious language.

Siddhi Khairiyat Khan killed Kondaji

As the day comes, the mines were planted, and Kondaji Farzand's colleagues were in the sea carrying sails. Shambhu Raje came with the army of 20000 Marathas & waiting at the shore of the sea for the indication of Kondaji.

But unfortunately, Kondaji was found red-handed when he was about to blast the Ammunition storage of Janjira.

Sidhhi Khairiyat Khan came to know about this plan of Shambhu Raje, he became very angry and ordered to cut the head of Kondaji & sent his head to Shambhu Raje as a gift. Siddhi himself killed Kondaji Farzand & sent his head to Shambhu Raje, also sent the message to go back don't you dare to attack Janjira.

All the Marathas on Janjira were killed. One of the Maratha chiefs survived. He told Shambhu Raje the fact. The Shambhu Raje was shocked.

Kondaji Farzand was a brave and noble chief but he was very close to him. Tears came up in the king's eyes. But it was not the time to get emotional.

The King Shambhu Raje decided to attack the fort so that Kondaji's sacrifice will be worthwhile. They attacked Janjira with an army of twenty thousand and three hundred ships.

Setu by Chhatrapati Sambhaji Maharaj

After this, under the leadership of Sambhaji, the Marathas attacked the fort from all sides. Siddhi made a great resistance from the ships with his guns.

Then Chhatrapati Sambhaji Maharaj's cannons started firing from the shore. Maratha's guns started firing.

The cannons of the Marathas were reaching the fort. Siddhi's big Shishmahal was shattered. Everything was going in the favor of Shambhu Raje. But at the crucial time, the sea came to Janjira's help. The sea was tidal.

The Marathas began to move backward. But Shambhu Raje did not stop. They decided to build a bridge across the sea. Work began; the bridge began to take shape. Construction was extremely dangerous, difficult, and expensive. They took the material from the hills of Rajapuri to build a path in the sea. After taking all materials, the bridge was started to build.

Just like Lord Shri Ram built the Ram Bridge to invade Lanka, Chhatrapati Sambhaji Maharaj built a bridge of 800 meters in the rising sea to capture the Janjira fort.

Janjira fort was 90% damaged in the battle between Siddhi & Shambhu Raje.

Aurangzeb & British helps Sidhhi

Aurangzeb made a move, realizing that if Janjira fell into the hands of the Marathas, the Sambhaji's kingdom (swarajya) would become more powerful. Aurangzeb sent a chief named Hasan Ali Khan to march on Swarajya.

Hasan Ali, the chief of Aurangzeb, had started marching towards Raigad via Kalyan-Bhiwandi with an army of 40,000 men.

While the bridge was about half-built, news came that Aurangzeb had sent troops to Raigad to destroy the Swarajya. Sambhaji had to give up the Janjira campaign partially to resist the Mughal army.

In mid-1682, the Mughals dispatched a military mission against the military Maratha. Kalyan-Bhiwandi was assaulted by a Mughal armed force.

The city is said to have been torched by the Mughal head Hasan Ali Khan Kalyan-Bhiwandi in the long stretch of Magh (likely January 1682) and Back. It is fascinating to discover that the British covertly provided during this mission Ammo to Mughal general Hasan Ali Khan.

The mission against Sambhaji was preceded - which implies tempestuous circumstances and the British lost exchange and business.

It ought to be noticed that the East India Company was fundamentally an exchanging substance, with the primary goal of gigantic benefits through exchange and business.

By using guerrilla tactics, King Shambhu Raje attacked Hasan Ali Khan & they cut his hand. Chhatrapati Sambhaji Maharaj roars & said to Hasan Ali Khan,

"Go & tell the Aurangzeb that the son of Chhatrapati Shivaji Maharaj is capable to protect the Swarajya".

Don't you dare to invade swarajya?

Remember the name, Sambhaji Chhatrapati Sambhaji.

Withdrawal of Janjira Expedition

Before Chhatrapati Sambhaji could think of any elective intend to seek after his military furthermore, maritime tasks against Janjira in a more beneficial manner, he got knowledge about the development of the Mughal powers nearby Maratha region.

It involved grave worry on two records. One, the defiant Mughal ruler Akbar was expanded cordiality by the Marathas; furthermore, considering the responsibility of an enormous body of the Maratha troops to Janjira, the Maratha protections were powerless and presented to the adversary from the landward side.

Simultaneously, the Mughals, with the point of the obliteration of the Deccan realms, were pushing forward in immense volumes. Sambhaji in this way couldn't change the destiny of the Maratha Swaraiya for Janjira.

Simultaneously, he was smart enough not to alleviate Janjira of the Maratha pressure. He organized the continuation of the attack of Janjira with a significant number of troops and a portion of his most capable administrators like Govindrao Kate, Daulat Khan, Kavaji Mohammad, Govindji Kanho, Govindji Jadhav, Santaji Pavla, and 400 unflinching officers under the order of Dadaji Prabhu.

In this manner, King Sambhaji needed to pull out himself from the Janjira campaign which he had by and by administered and coordinated for quite a while.

After the takeoff of Chhatrapati Sambhaji Maharaj, the excess Maratha unforeseen kept on making endeavors to obliterate, get close and land at Janjira however missed the mark concerning imprint and lost numerous decided Maratha officers in this interaction.

With the coming of a storm, it was not; at this point suitable for the Marathas to proceed at the ocean subsequently the endeavor was canceled during the pinnacle of the rainstorm.

After that Siddhi & not even any of his brothers did not try to interfere in the Maratha territory. Remains of a half-built bridge can still be seen at Janjira. Again, it was Maratha Victory.

"सभी सुखो को छोड के वो स्वराज्य के लिये खडा था,
सागर मे सेतू का संकल्प प्रभु श्रीराम के बाद बस शंभु ने ही किया था |"

Chapter X

KING SHAMBHU & CHIKKADEVRAJA

Taking advantage of the Mughal crisis on the Marathas, Chikka Devaraya from the south India started infiltrating the Swarajya. Chhatrapati Sambhaji Maharaj sent his messenger to Chikka Devaraya. Chikka Devaraya insulted the messenger of Swarajya in his court.

This time, however, Chhatrapati Sambhaji Maharaj decided to attack Mysore. He also sought help from Jinji's cousin-uncle Ekoji Raje.

Maratha-Mysore War

Maratha-Mysore War (1682) was a sequence of battles fought between the Maratha Empire and the Kingdom of Mysore in Southern India. Both powers had been looking to advantage supremacy in Southern India which led to this conflict & also Chikka Devaraya was secretly helping the Aurangzeb in the opposition of Chhatrapati Sambhaji Maharaj.

Chhatrapati Sambhaji Maharaj's grandfather Shahaji Raje Bhosale had conquered territories in the states of Karnataka. Mohammed Adil Shah, Sultan of Bijapur granted him the Jagir of Bangalore. This turned into the entry of the Marathas in Southern India. Chhatrapati Shivaji Maharaj had established Maratha territories in Southern India in his two-year-long South India campaign of 1676–78.

The Maratha Sardar Harji Raje Mahadik additionally defeated the Mysore general Kumaraiya. Both forces had tried to subdue each different ensuing in a stalemate. Chhatrapati Sambhaji Maharaj also attempted to shape a Deccan alliance against the Mughal Emperor Aurangzeb. Chikkadevaraya allied himself with Aurangzeb & captured some of the Maratha Sardars.

This enraged Chhatrapati Sambhaji Maharaj and he attacked the Kingdom of Mysore in June 1682 along with his allies Qutb Shahi dynasty and the Nayakas of Hukkeri. Allied forces reached Banavar in June 1682.

To counter the allied navy at Banavar, Chikkadevaraya left Mysore along with his robust contingent of 15,000 expert archers. He wanted to assault before the allies settled in the vicinity. Both aspects organized for the struggle. And the warfare started out with small skirmishes.

Soon, Chikkadevaraya found out that the allied forces did now not have archers. He organized his archers in a semicircular formation and started showering arrows at the allied navy.

Chikka Devaraya decided to stop the Marathas before they reached the region of Mysore. The Maratha army was greeted with a huge barrage of arrows.

The archers of Mysore shot long and metal arrows and wounded the Marathas with life threatening wounds. Chhatrapati Sambhaji Maharaj decided to retreat to avoid extra casualties and he retreated closer to Thanjavur.

Story of Bullet Proof Jacket

Chhatrapati Sambhaji Maharaj rested close to Thanjavur for 20 days. He obtained extra reinforcements from Hukkeri and Golconda. His uncle Ekoji Raje also joined forces with him.

Chhatrapati Sambhaji Maharaj decided to draw chikka Devaraya away from their stronghold to flat plains close to Madurai. He determined to attack and besiege the town of Tiruchirapalli. The weakened Nayaka of Madurai, Chokkanatha Nayak lived on the fortress. Still, the town had robust defenses and a formidable Mysore garrison in the town and on the castle.

Chhatrapati Sambhaji Maharaj desired to defeat the prevalence of Mysore archers. During their rest time Chhatrapati Sambhaji Maharaj ordered all of the cobblers from neighboring villages and made leather-based arrow-evidence jackets for his entire army.

The Marathas made bows and arrows using the available local wood. These leather-based jackets were coated with a layer of oil to avoid arrows from getting stuck within the jackets.

Chhatrapati Sambhaji Maharaj also accrued the abundantly to be had elephants from the surrounding area. He ordered all of the boatmen from the close by villages to collect with his navy. Three hundred archers of the Maratha navy have been organized to hearth lit arrows during the attack.

Tiruchirapalli was based on the opposite of the Kaveri river bank. At the sunrise, the Maratha forces crossed the river by use of the boats accrued from nearby villages.

The unexpected attack of the Marathas surprised the Mysore defenders; they started out showering arrows at the Maratha Army.

The archers of Mysore used bows and arrows of a much stronger and better quality than the Marathas; but this time the Maratha leather jackets provided powerful safety from the arrows from the Mysore bowmen.

Elephants broke the main doorways inside the meanwhile and fierce warfare ensued at the streets of Tiruchirappalli. Marathas captured the city by the night but the Tiruchirapalli Rock Fort turned into still controlled by using the Mysore military.

Meanwhile, Chokkanatha Nayak died at the citadel. Chhatrapati Sambhaji Maharaj with a force of 10,000 laid sieges to the fort after 10 days. The Marathas again adopted comparable methods to defeat Mysore archers.

The Maratha archers accurately struck lit arrows on the ammunitions depot within the citadel resulting in a huge explosion and crumble of the wall. The Marathas soon entered and captured the fortress.

The Marathas sacked Tiruchirapalli. Pashankot of Tiruchirappalli fell into the hands of the Marathas. It has been noted that this victory changed into a fulfillment factor of Chhatrapati Sambhaji's navy intelligence.

King Sambhaji's Victory

The defeat at Tiruchirappalli dealt a intense blow to Chikkadevaraya. Several of his allies joined Chhatrapati Sambhaji Maharaj.

He captured numerous fortresses inside the northern provinces of Madurai. He also held all of the provinces of Dharmapuri and other neighboring territories.

Chikkadevaraya entered negotiations with Chhatrapati Sambhaji Maharaj and taken a stop to the struggle by using paying the tribute. According to Maratha assets, a treaty turned into signed at Srirangapatna in which he paid 1 Crore Honas as a heat tribute to Chhatrapati Sambhaj Maharaj.

However, this became a brief give up and the conflicts persisted within the following years.

The Jesuit letter of 1682 describes the precarious position of Chikka Devaraja, "The energy of the king of Mysore begins to develop susceptible because, violently attacked in his own dominions by the troops of Chhatrapati Sambhaji, and he can't maintain and enhance the armies he had sent to those nations."

The brother-in-law of Chhatrapati Sambhaji Raje in Karnataka Harji Raje Mahadik had shielded the Karnataka over the years.

"दुश्मन को हराने के लिये किया था जिसने गनिमी कावा,
वो धगधगती आग सा शिव का था छावा"

Chapter XI

PORTUGUESE & BRITISH

Portuguese of Goa tried to help Aurangzeb even after convincing them by Marathas, but then Chhatrapati Sambhaji Maharaj had to go to Goa on his own. The story of the unspeakable atrocities perpetrated by the Portuguese on the citizens of Goa reached Chhatrapati Sambhaji Raje. Chhatrapati Sambhaji Raje was requested to free the people of swarajya from Portuguese oppression.

Then Chhatrapati Sambhaji Maharaj marched on Goa with a few of his Army. The Portuguese were shaken by the Shambhu Raje's unique way of attacking & moving like a storm.

Chhatrapati Sambhaji Raje himself was at the forefront of the Goa campaign. In just one month, he captured three-quarters of Goa.

The Portuguese ruled Goa for the last century. They had built strong fortifications around the city of Panaji. The governor of Goa, County de Alvor, had many guns ready for self-defense.

That is why Chhatrapati Sambhaji Maharaj knew that invading Goa and attacking the Portuguese would be a great feat.

That is why Chhatrapati Sambhaji Raje was planning to take this governor out of Goa and attack him. Fonda fort near Goa was in the possession of the Marathas.

Chhatrapati Sambhaji Raje decided to force the Portuguese of Goa to come to this fort.

Guerilla warfare by King Sambhaji

According to the plan, Shambhu Raje started spreading rumors in Goa from his people that "Chhatrapati Sambhaji Maharaj has brought a treasure of Rs 5 crore to Fonda fort near Goa, along with a lot of ammunition."

At this time Chhatrapati Sambhaji Maharaj was at Raigad fort. The governor knew the news. The governor knew that the fortifications of the Fonda fort were not strong. And there aren't many troops on the fort. He thought that there were a few Maratha on the Fonda fort, and the Chhatrapati of the Marathas was not even close.

That is why he feels strong and started attacking Fonda fort.

Governor County de Alvor got stuck in Chhatrapati Sambhaji Raje's guerrilla warfare. He took 5,000 Portuguese troops with him and attacked Fonda fort.

It was night when the governor reached the fort with his Portuguese troops. It was dark. But he decided not to wait till morning, to attack the fort at night. He climbed the fort at night.

Battle of Fonda

Maratha Chieftain Yesaji Kank and Krishnaji Kank were the father and son on the fort. The Portuguese mounted cannon on a hill in front of the fort. These firearms were long-range. From this hill, he was firing cannons at the Fonda fort of Marathas. At the same time, Portuguese soldiers were firing.

The battle lasted until the next day when a bastion of the ramparts of the Fonda fort collapsed. The governor was pleased to see that.

He ordered his troops to enter the fort. But not a single Portuguese soldier was ready to advance in the face of the Maratha attack from the fort. But nothing happened to him before the governor's order.

Then some Portuguese advanced and came near the fort. Stones were hurled from the fort. Then the Portuguese retreated.

But still, for 4 days in a row, artillery was firing on the fort from that hill. The real situation was that one day the fort would fall into the hands of the Portuguese. The Portuguese governor was mad with joy.

He had seen the Portuguese flag on the Fonda fort. The Marathas on the fort were fighting for the fort by betting their lives as per the order of Chieftain Yesaji Kank.

Chhatrapati Shambhu attacked on Portuguese

And so on. From a distance, the dust began to appear from some distance, chants could be heard, "Har Har Mahadev, Chhatrapati Shivaji Maharaj ki Jai, Chhatrapati Sambhaji Maharaj ki Jai".

All the Marathas on the Fonda fort stood on stilts and bastions and looked there... every moment the noise was increasing. King Shambhu himself had come to the aid of Yesaji Kank. Seeing this, they were also responded from the fort, slogans started rising from the fort, "Chhatrapati Sambhaji Maharaj ki Jai".

Chhatrapati Sambhaji Maharaj, his cavalry, infantry, all the army had come to keep the fort of Fonda, to taste the dust of defeat to the Portuguese.

The Portuguese, however, noticed this, but then their scars faded, and their fears were shattered. Till now, the governor had only heard the stories of Chhatrapati Sambhaji Maharaj's prowess. Seeing him in front of him today, the governor was scared and exhausted. He immediately ordered his troops to retreat. The Portuguese army was also waiting for the same order. The Marathas on the fort was very happy to see this view.

Count De Alvor, the Governor of Goa, was released by the Marathas. The invasion of Goa by the Marathas was so severe that the Governor of Goa had to move his capital from Panaji to Marma Goa.

The Marathi people of Goa were very happy to see Chhatrapati Sambhaji Maharaj and his descendants attacking the Govekar Portuguese. Many people in Goa had endured years of persecution and oppression by the Portuguese.

Today, many years later, they were enjoying freedom.

In retaliation for the demolition of several temples in Goa by the Portuguese in the last few years, some Hindus in Goa came together and attacked a Christian church in Goa, setting it on fire and setting it on fire.

Chhatrapati Sambhaji Raje, who was proud of his own religion and had respect for other religions, did not like this news. He further addressed the crowd and said,

"This Swarajya is established by our Abasaheb and is not based on hatred of anyone's religion." Chhatrapati Sambhaji Maharaj ordered,

Chhatrapati Sambhaji Maharaj converted some Hindus who had converted to Christianity. He opposed to changing of religion forcefully and gave some faith of not being attacked by Portuguese furthermore for changing of religion.

King Sambhaji's Victory

The governor had already left Panaji, convinced that it was impossible to defeat Chhatrapati Sambhaji Maharaj. He feared that Shambhu Raje would one day conquer the whole of Goa. So he decided to save his life by making a pact with Chhatrapati Sambhaji Maharaj.

That is why the governor had sent his lawyer to Shambhu Raje. A few days later, Sambhaji Raje held talks with the Portuguese. And they came back to Raigad.

The situation for the colonists became so dire that the Portuguese viceroy, Francisco de Távora, Counte de Alvor went with his remaining supporters to the cathedral where the crypt of Saint Francis Xavier was kept, where they prayed for deliverance.

The viceroy had the casket opened, and gave the saint's body his baton, royal credentials, and a letter asking the saint's support. Chhatrapati Sambhaji's Goa campaign was checked by the arrival of the Mughal army and navy in January 1684, forcing him to withdraw the expedition of Goa.

Maratha-Portuguese Conflicts

Portuguese force arose as an amazing naval force in the sixteenth century. During the time of both Chhatrapati Shivaji Maharaj and Chhatrapati Sambhaji Maharaj, the Maratha naval powers were efficient and they set up naval bases in the seaside zones of Maharashtra.

The Maratha naval force was solid, constructed, and had its arrangement of building maritime bases.

Like Chhatrapati Shivaji Maharaj the Great, Chhatrapati Sambhaji Raje additionally sought after an approach of reinforcing maritime force. The Portuguese were solid in Goa and they were extending their impact in the Konkan district of Maharashtra.

Asserting interest was unavoidable because Portuguese powers had held onto a few maritime ports to build their exchange and business. They focused on crude materials and related things

Exchange, Chhatrapati Sambhaji's severe strict exchange and trade rules were disturbing the Portuguese and they were searching in any capacity whatsoever for struggle. Chhatrapati Sambhaji Raje was consistently a tycoon just as mindful of the Portuguese plan of hostility and assault. Alongside the development of his exchange, his transformation during the Chhatrapati Sambhaji's time frame and his atrocities on the neighborhood Hindu people group prompted the Portuguese and Maratha clashes.

Chhatrapati Sambhaji Maharaj was more effective against Portuguese force than Chhatrapati Shivaji's approaches since his arrangements were better. Chhatrapati Sambhaji's endeavors to control the extension of Portugal depended on the cautious and cognizant endeavors of the ruler.

The different stages and occasions of the Portuguese battle are significant brilliant sections in the vocation of Chhatrapati Sambhaji Maharaj.

He was against the Portuguese and continuously set the edge on them. Chhatrapati Sambhaji's prosperity demonstrated his potential as well as made a sensation of dread and fear in his enemy.

However, the Portuguese again raised their heads. Then the Chhatrapati Sambhaji Maharaj made the Portuguese permanent silent. History records that after the invasion of Chhatrapati Sambhaji Raje, the Portuguese remained silent for many years.

Relations with British (Topikar)

Like Chhatrapati Shivaji Maharaj, Chhatrapati Sambhaji Raje was very much aware of the strategies of the English ambassadors who were utilizing segment and state arrangements.

Chhatrapati Sambhaji's approaches against the English depended on waiting and watching. He additionally opposed the approach of separation and rule against the Portuguese and English.

They depended on the approach of helping out the British and battling the British as opposed to the British which was more goal-oriented. So Chhtrapati Sambhaji vanquished as well as battled against them with valiance and ability.

Chhatrapati Sambhaji's approach against the British depended on the interests of the state. The cognizance in this relationship had the option to enter him. To ensure exchange and business benefits for the Maratha realm, he attempted to help one unfamiliar force against another.

The arrangement and choices taken by Chhatrapati Sambhaji Maharaj have been concentrated by the Portuguese and the British in their manufacturing plants. Every one of these variables can be appropriately inspected to analyze the various elements of Maratha's international strategy.

Like Chhatrapati Shivaji Maharaj, King Sambhaji had the option to devise the correct methodology dependent on the correct choice. Every one of these issues has been painstakingly analyzed to adequately center the Maratha relationship with the English East India Company. Zones of contention and collaboration were mostly identified with costly Maharashtra up to Bombay and Karwar. The various elements of the Maratha-English battle can be concentrated based on the assets accessible as processing plant records which can be deliberately archived here.

Siddhi of Janjira and the English East India Company were vital participants in the contemporary strategic maneuver of the decade. He was making issues and strains for the Marathas by muddling a few issues. Chhatrapati Sambhaji Maharaj was very much aware of current realities and circumstances around him and he managed the two of them deliberately and strategically.

Maratha-English Agreement

Like his father, Chhatrapati Sambhaji Maharaj needed to battle contrary to the standards of Janjira. Chhatrapati Shivaji Maharaj assembled Khanderi fortress while his son Chhatrapati Sambhaji Raje fabricated Andari and Dandarajpuri.

To control the accomplishment, Chhatrapati Sambhaji Raje wanted to assault Bombay. To counter the Siddhi & English coalition, Shambhu Raje becomes friends with the Arabs and prevails about finding support from them. The organization workplaces in Surat and Bombay were playing a twofold game.

At the point when Siddhi and the Mughals attached Bombay, the British had no chance to get of becoming a close acquaintance with the Chhatrapati Sambhaji Maharaj, which made ready out of the emergency. After 1683, the English-Maratha arrangement was agreed upon. Chhatrapati Sambhaji's depiction of insight in exchange, business and military collaboration, Chhatrapati Sambhaji had built up the Maratha Navy, and King Sambhaji's solid help made conceivable the ascent of Kanhoji Angre as the top of the Maratha Navy.

Chhatrapati Shambhu Raje had neighborly relations with the French and had gotten arms and ammo from them. Be that as it may, when they were building strongholds, Shambhu Raje cautioned against them.

In any case, the post was permitted to arrive at a specific stature in the wake of getting remuneration. The Dutch were unsettled and began assaulting the Portuguese. Maratha-English relations depended on irreconcilable circumstances. The English had entered the western part during the East India Company period and were utilized in any event, during the time of Aurangzeb relying upon the strategy of segment and rule.

Shambhu Raje was exceptionally cautious while managing with the English, similar to his father. The English public was shrewd and strategic and the Marathas must be cautious while managing them. Sambhaji Raje followed a similar approach. Like Chhatrapati Shivaji Maharaj, Shambhu Raje was consistently mindful while working in the English East India Company.

The English force was cognizant and consistently careful in managing the Maratha realm and the King Sambhaji were a lot mindful of their strategies and they were utilizing the English and the Portuguese against one another. His cautious technique profited both.

"सामने था सिद्धी, औरंगझेब , फिरंगी ..था चिक्कदेवराजा,
उन सबपे भारी पडा था बस एक ही शंभूराजा |"

Chapter XII

BETRAYAL WITH KING SHAMBHU

The Mughal emperor Aurangzeb tried his all tactics against the Maratha kingdom, but his all activities went in vain. He failed to get a hold of the Maratha kingdom during the first five years of the attack. That's why he decided to attack on Adilshah of Vijapur. He defeated Adilshah Sultan and Kutubshah in the years 1686 and 1687 respectively.

Aurangzeb was helpless during the fight with Maratha, but he got success in the south against these two states of Adilshah and Kutubshah.

Due to these incidents, he got some belief that he can capture Maratha king also. He was very angry with Shambhuraje; he wanted his crown to be on his head back. At any cost, he wanted to defeat Shambhuraje.

But in the Maharashtra region, he found it very difficult to defeat Chhatrapati Sambhaji Maharaj in a straight fight. So wisely he decided to attract some Maratha Sardar with his power.

He started a campaign against Shambhuraje. Those who were in oppose of Chhatrapati Sambhaji Maharaj, those who doesn't like the decisions of Chhatrapati, those who were loath on Shambhuraje, those who wanted to be a part of the Mughal army joins the Aurangzeb's camp.

Shaikh Nizam aka Muqarrab Khan

Aurangzeb had sent his chieftain towards swarajya with 25000 Army. The name of that chieftain was Muqarrab Khan aka Shaikh Nizam, he marched towards the Maratha kingdom with his army in the Kolhapur region. His main aim was to capture the toughest panhala fort.

Meanwhile, Aurangzeb sent a letter to him mentioning that, rather than attacking Panhala go and attack on Sambhaji and try to capture him as he is not on Raigad at this time.

There are internal conflicts between Sambhaji and Shirke's of Shringarpur.

He is not aware of our army and activities go and captured the Maratha king.

Muqarrab khan was very shrewd; he spread his spies across the Maratha region. He took the help of regional people to find the roads of the Sahyadri hills.

Conflicts between Shirke and Kavi Kalash

Maratha kingdom was fighting with Mughals with a brave heart. Some of the chieftains of swarajya were not happy with the governing of Chhatrapati Sambhaji Maharaj; Shirke's of shringarpur was one of them.

Some of them left the swarajya and joined the Mughal camp. The rebellion act was started against the Maratha King.

There are some evidence in Jedhe Shakavali, that there was estrangement between Kavi Kalash and Shirke. In 1688, the conflicts between these two were at their peak. Kavi Kalash was the Best friend of Chhatrapati Sambhaji Maharaj. He went to protect his friend at that time.

This incident leads to rebel of Shirke, also Shirke were demanding the heritage, the pieces of some lands from the reigns of Chhatrapati Shivaji Maharaj.

But it was against the rules of Swarajya, hence neither Chhatrapati Shivaji Maharaj accept it nor Chhatrapati Sambhaji Maharaj.

Aurangzeb pointed out this opportunity to get Shirke and some other Maratha Chieftains in his camp. With the help of these people, he wanted to reach Raigad and defeat the Shambhuraje.

Muqqarab khan took these people with him; they show the path from Kolhapur to Sangameshwar. Spies of Muqqarab khan inform him about the location of Chhatrapati Sambhaji Maharaj. Muqarrab was finding his path very secretly.

Muqarrab Khan makes way towards Shambhu Raje

Shambhu Raje and his friend Kavi Kalash were discussing with their Mavala and few selected people at Sangameshwar.

Aurangzeb was angry that his son Akbar had resorted under Chhatrapati Sambhaji Maharaj to hide from Mughal emperor. Chhatrapati Sambhaji Maharaj solved the problems of the people of the surrounding villages. The Mughal chief Mukarrab

Khan was informed by some insidious traitors that Shambhu Raje was in Sangameshwar village in his own Swarajya.

There was a very little army with Chhatrapati Sambhaji Maharaj at that time, of course, we were in our own state and he was in his father-in-law's territory so he ignored it. His father, Chhatrapati Shivaji Maharaj, had taught him to be careful at every moment from his childhood.

अखंड सावध असावे, दुश्चित कदापि नसावे,
तजविजा करीत बसावे, एकांत स्थळी |

It means one should always be careful & never be mischievous. But, Chhatrapati Sambhaji Maharaj never thought that people from Swarajya will betrayal against him & that too from his in laws people.

Muqarrab Khan was marching towards Samgameshvar with the help of Swarajya's traitors. Siddhi, British, Portuguesue, Dutch, Chhikadevaraya & other enemies of Shambhu Raje were more confident when Aurangzeb helped them all in campaigns against the Chhatrapati Sambhaji Maharaj. That's why Shambhu Raje was planning to destroy the Aurangzeb's emperor; they were aggressive on that point.

Sarsenapati Maloji Baba Ghorpade

Muqarrab Khan attacked the Maratha army from behind. Chhatrapati Sambhaji Maharaj had an idea of the enemy but he did not even dream that his own people would betray him. And that is why the betrayal of our own people caused a great crisis to the Marathas.

Sarsenapati Maloji Baba Ghorpade was with the Shambhu Raje. He requested Chhatrapati Sambhaji Maharaj to leave that place immediately. But Shambhu Raje was not one of the fugitives.

He told Maloji Baba that he would not go, endangering the lives of the Maratha brothers who were with him. With the roar of Har Har Mahadev, the Shambhu raje counter-attacked on Muqarrab Khan's army.

Maloji Baba was worried about the king Sambhaji. There was a lot of enemy army; they knew we would be defeated there.

Maloji Baba said to Shambhu Raje, "I request you to go ahead; I will stop the Mughal army here. Please go Shambhu Raje go"

Hearing those words, Shambhu Raje remembered the incident of Pavankhind (Ghodkhind) when Bajiprabhu Deshpande insisted

Chhatrapati Shivaji Maharaj to move towards Vishalgad. There were tears in the eyes of Shambhu Raje.

A fierce war broke out between the Mughals and the Marathas. The Shambhu Raje assumed the form of Rudra, just as the cataclysm came when Lord Shiva Shankara opened his third eye, as if the time had come upon the Mughals.

The sword of King Shambhu Raje was running like lightning against the Mughal army. The Marathas got more strength and power when they saw that their king was raining fire on the enemy for them even when their soldiers were less.

The Marathas, burning with hatred, fell on the enemy. On the one hand, the Shambhu Raje used their power to kill the Mughal army.

On the other hand, Maloji Baba Ghorpade was fighting stubbornly, while Muqarrab Khan called in more troops and attacked Maloji Baba.

A huge war broke out between Maloji Baba and Muqarrab Khan.

Maloji baba was tired now, despite his age, he fought with Muqarrab Khan. And finally Maloji baba died a heroic death.

Maloji Baba collapsed and fell down, Shambhu Raje saw him. Maloji Baba was telling Chhatrapati Sambhaji Maharaj to get out of here, at the last moment he paid his last respects to the king.

Chhatrapati Sambhaji Raje cried, the Marathas were upset to see that their commander had died. Everyone urged the king to leave.

The Kavi Kalash and Shambhu Raje were advancing slowly from Sangmeshvar but the enemy army was growing in front.

Muqarrab captured Shambhu Raje & Kavi Kalash

The poet Kalash now began to fight with hatred. He took Maratha army with him to support Chhatrapati Sambhaji Maharaj. They begged the king to go ahead and fight. But now was not the time to leave.

Mughal troops attacked from all sides. Saying that Maloji Baba, we will not allow your sacrifice to go in vain, the Marathas became stubborn.

There was a stormy war, the Maratha soldiers were tired of this sudden attack and after fighting for a long time, but everyone was fighting till their last breath.

Suddenly an arrow came from behind and hit the poet Kalash. Kalash stopped for a while, his legs were bruised.

Chhatrapati Sambhaji Maharaj saw it and ran to his friend. They Killed the Mughal soldiers there. Seeing the manner in which Shambhu Raje was fighting, the Mughal soldiers had no clue & idea to stop him.

Muqarrab Khan had never seen such a brave and mighty king in his entire life.

"The king who was fighting against the Mughals in front of him was the same king who had made to leave the throne of Aurangzeb's Delhi, who had defeated Siddhi, the English, the Portuguese, the Dutch, Chikkadevaraya, and the Mughals for 10 years."

This is the same king for whom 5 lakh troops had come to Deccan. So many people for one person, so this is not even a simple king. Once upon a time there was such a person; an invincible Chhatrapati Sambhaji Maharaj.

Seeing the incarnation of Rudra of the Shambhu Raje, the Mughal soldiers were fleeing.

Seeing this, Muqarrab Khan ordered the soldiers to go and attack Chhatrapati Sambhaji all together.

Even 100 to 200 people were not going to catch Shambhu Raja.

Chhatrapati Sambhaji Maharaj was surrounded from all sides. Now there were weapons to fight, but there were many enemies in front. The king of Swarajya was captured by the Mughals in danger.

The Mughals did not even have the courage to tie the hands of the Chhatarapati Sambhaji Maharaj. Only the Shambhu Raje looked with their eyes that the soldier would go back 5 steps.

At last the attack took place; the chain was thrown on the body of Shambhu Raje. The whole body was chained, Muqarrab Khan laughed out loud. Now Aurangzeb will be happy with me, I caught his biggest enemy. His laughing voice, however, gave only one sorrow to the Marathas. Screams spread everywhere, news spread that our king was captured by the Mughals.

The Marathas fought but now it was too late. Muqarrab Khan took the Shambhu Raje to Bahadurgad (Dharmaveergad) by the route shown by Shirke's. He had such orders from Aurangzeb.

The moment he heard the news, he went crazy with joy. There was a fearful silence in the Swarajya that would never be filled.

Chapter XIII

11 MARCH 1689

Aurangzeb saw King Sambhaji in front of him and he came down from his place. And said that, for whom I came to the Deccan with such a large army, for whom I threw the crown from my head, for whom I have waited so long to be killed, Sambha (King Sambhaji) is present in front of me today.

Oh, Allah, how can be I thankful to you! Aurangzeb was very happy to have King Sambhaji as prisoner. Everyone was amazed to see Aurangzeb kneeling in front of Shambhuraje to thank God (Allah).

Chhatrapati Sambhaji Maharaj forced the Mughal emperor to get from the Mughal Samrat's seat and sit down in front of him.

Poet Kalash & Aurangzeb

Poet Kalash at Shree Dharmaveer gad (fort) (Bahadurgad) Poem recited in front of Aurangzeb on 15th February 1689. After seeing that Aurangzeb has kneeled down to Chhatrapati Sambhaji Maharaj, Kalash started one poem in a very brave manner.

King Sambhaji praised Kavi Kalash for coming up with such a poem on such a difficult occasion, it was not just a poem but it was a insult of Mughal emperor Aurangzeb.

यावन रावन की सभा संभू बंध्यो बजरंग ।

लहू लसत सिंदूर सम खूब खेल्यो रनरंग ।।

ज्यो रबि छबि लखतही नथीत होत बदरंग ।

त्यो तव तेज निहारके तखत त्यजो अवरंग ।।

Meaning:

Like Lord Hanuman, Chhatrapati Sambhaji Raja has been taken captive in front of Aurangzeb (Ravana). Chhatrapati Sambhaji's bloodied limbs look like Hanumanta's torn limbs due to playing immense war. As the fireflies fade away when the sun rises in the sky, Shambhu Raje due to your glory Aurangzeb has given up his desire & wishes.

By hearing this poem, Aurangzeb got angry on Kalash & he ordered to his army to take both King Sambhaji & Kalash to the Jail (Prison).

King Shambhu & Muqarrab Khan

In the prison, the hands and feet of King Shambhu Raje and Kavi Kalash were tied with chains.

King Shambhuraje asked Kavi Kalash, why you took risk of your life for me?

Kavi Kalash said, "King, I will give this support of our friendship till my last breath." Even if death comes, let us face it together, we lived together, let us die for you now.

Soon, Muqarrab Khan arrived.

Muqarrab Khan asked King Shambhu, why don't you apologize in front of the emperor?

Say Sorry to him for your crimes against Mughal Empire, then Badshah Aurangzeb will forgive you. Otherwise your death is final.

Shambhu Raje aggressively shouted on Khan, "I will not apologize to your king."

Muqarrab Khan,

This Sahyadri and Maharashtra are ours.

You can kill us today, but remember your grave will be dug here tomorrow. So be ready for the circumstances.

Muqarrab Khan got panicked and took two steps back and went back to Army camp.

King Shambhu & Aurangzeb

Next Day, Muqarrab khan presented both King Shambhu & Kavi Kalash in front of Aurangzeb. Aurangzeb was shocked by looking at King Sambhaji; he wondered how can be someone as strong as Sambhaji.

There was no regret in the eyes of Chhatrapati Sambhaji Maharaj.

Aurangzeb again asked to King Shambhu to do not make eye contact to him, these eyes irritating me.

He said, I still rememberd your childhood presence at Agra, everyone took their eye contact my feet but only you kept the eye contact with me infront of everyone.

No changes at all! Right now you are the same, bow down to me Sambha, bow down

Shambhu Raje replied, never ... even if death comes, but these eyes will never bow to you.

Now Aurangzeb was literally stunned by hearing this, he was thinking exactly who is the prisoner?

This Sambha or me? How can he talk to me like this?

He calmly said, listen Sambha. I will forgive your all the crimes which you have performed against our Mughal empire.

Just answer to my some questions & then I will make you free from this chains & prison.

King Shambhu started to Laugh.

He said to whom you are talking these non sense things? I know even if I answer to your questions, you are going to kill me. Then why should I tell you anything.

You killed your father, you killed your brothers for this Mughal Empires crown & you are talking about forgiveness.

Literally?

Aurangzeb asked, tell Sambha.

Where you have kept all the treasury & gold of Swarajya?

Who all are there with you from Mughal Kingdom? Tell the names of Mughal betrayers.

And lastly convert your religion, come in Islam, your life will change & you will stay happy.

Chhatrapati Sambhaji Maharaj calmly answered, see Aurangzeb, and listen carefully.

"I can not say anything about the treasury. My all treasury is my Marathas & the forts which have been built on the sacrifice of my all Maratha army. You can not take this from me & no one else can!"

And talking about Mughal betrayers, I can take only one name. Your own Son Akbar.

"You are asking to change my Dharma (Religion), I will never change my Hindu Dharma. I had lived in past, I am living in current & will live my life in future also as Hindu, I will end my life in Hindu Dharma only. No one can force me to convert."

The whole Mughal court was shooked.

11 March 1689

The Mughal emperor Aurangzeb thought that Chhatrapati Sambhaji is rude & ruthless. He knew that he would never tell us where his treasure was. He will never change his religion.

He threatened that he will kill King Sambhaji and will attack on Raigad after killing him.

Then Shambhu Raje said, one day everyone is going to be dying!

This Chhatrapati Sambhaji will die a thousand times for the Swarajya and my motherland which is created by our Abasaheb (Chhatrapati Shivaji Maharaj).

But remember one thing, if I die, your grave will be dug here.

"Undoubtedly you can only kill my body, you can destroy it. But I am the Chhatrapati of this Hindustan, I am an idea which is in the minds of the people here; It will neither destroy by you nor by your next generations."

If this Sambhaji dies today, then millions of such Sambhajis will be born in the villages of Sahyadri.

Aurangzeb gets angry with King Shambhu, he did not like the way King Sambhaji was talking with him. He called Muqarrab khan & immediately ordered him to torture King Sambhaji & Kavi Kalash till their last breath.

Muqarrab Khan initiated the action on the orders of Aurangzeb. King Shambhu had a hot iron spear in both his eyes and his eyes were removed.

While doing so, the Mughals were scared, because King Shambhu Raje did not shout even after suffering so much. They stood quietly.

He remembered his father Chhatrapati Shivaji Maharaj.

The eyes in which my father had seen the future of Swarajya were destroyed today. Please forgive me Aabasaheb. Mughals cut the arms of King Shambhu; they remove the nails from his hand. Chhatrapati sambhaji Maharaj was brutally tortured by them for 40 days.

According to the historical records, King Shambhu was captured by Muqarrab Khan on 1 February 1689 & after 40 days of being tortured; finally, Aurangzeb had ordered to kill Chhatrapati Sambhaji Maharaj on 11 March 1689.

An Invincible King

Aurangzeb was devastated; he realized that the real defeat was mine. Despite all this trouble, Chhatrapati Sambhaji did not apologize to me; on the contrary, he faced death. I came to Deccan with my whole army just for this Chhatrapati Sambhaji Maharaj. I spent all my treasure.

We removed his eyes, but we are not seeing anything good, it seems that we are blind.

We cut his tongue, but my words are now stopped.

We broke his arm, but today my hands have become beggars due to the burden of defeats given by this Sambha.

For the last time, Chhatrapati Sambhaji Maharaj remembered his grandmother Rajmata Jijau & father Chhatrapati Shivaji Maharaj.

Along with King Shambhu, his friend Kavi Kalash was also brutally tortured & killed on the same day by the Mughals. King Shambhu was feeling very lucky to have such a loyal friend who can die with him & for him. On the orders of Aurangzeb, the Mughals cut the head of King Shambhu. Chhatrapati Sambhaji Maharaj ended their 32 years of life for the sake of the motherland.

Aurangzeb was questioning himself, from where did King Sambhaji get the strength to endure all this? If I had a son like him, I would have ruled not only India but the whole world.

He never bowed down to anyone in his entire life, even not in front of death, and remained invincible!

"काल की चौकट पे भी नहीं हुई जिसकी पराजय,
मौत भी नतमस्तक है, वो बस एक ही शंभु मृत्युंजय |"

Epilogue

In Maratha History, Chhatrapati Sambhaji Maharaj had played an important role in a significant part in the time of vulnerability and disturbance. After the demise of the great Chhatrapati Shivaji Maharaj, the Maratha state had a difficult stretch brimming with obscurity and loaded with unfriendly conditions. King Sambhaji needed to emerge from this whirl wind with extraordinary fortitude and certainty.

Chhatrapati Sambhaji Maharaj shines in Indian history based on his fortitude and penance. He had the option to set a motivating ideal over the number of Maratha supporters based on his solidarity and qualities.

Chhatrapati Sambhaji's profession as a fighter, as a King, and as an administrator is special, unparalleled, and unique. In a limited span to focus a decade, he had adequately engraved his impressions on the pathway of Indian history.

Another interpretation of Chhatrapati Sambhaji's career, accomplishments, and commitment has been made here in an intriguing way. The accomplishment of a ruler relies upon different variables on which premise he attempts to reshape conditions in support of himself.

Chhatrapati Sambhaji had the option to stamp on the wheel of time by raising quality execution and making sure about capacities of his own qualities. Chhatrapati Sambhaji Maharaj was extremely skilled in swordsmanship and other weapons. He used to fight with Lion with bare hands. As a result, nobody dared to fight against the Chhatrapati.

But unfortunately, Chhatrapati Sambhaji Maharaj and his advisors were captured by Muqarrab Khan, Mughal general. Chhatrapati Sambhaji was betrayed by his own family members; as a result, he was caught at Sangameshwar in February 1689.

Many of the historians are confused about how Chhatrapati Sambhaji Maharaj was captured in 1689 AD. The situation was so unpredictable that unfortunately no one can say for sure what exactly happened.

The confrontation of Chhatrapati Sambhaji Maharaj and Kavi Kalash vary according to many sources. But the fact that they were tortured and killed brutally by Emperor Aurangzeb is true. Thus on 11 March 1689, Chhatrapati Sambhaji Maharaj was killed at Vadhu-Tulapur near Pune.

When Chhatrapati Sambhaji Maharaj was imprisoned, he remembered his Late Father Chhatrapati Shivaji Maharaj and Goddess Bhavani. The King Sambhaji was entitled as Dharmaveer, and today he is referred as Dharmaveer Chhatrapati Sambhaji Maharaj.

Prince Rajaram Maharaj was crowned as the Maratha Chhatrapati after his brother, Chhatrapati Sambhaji Maharaj's death.

Bibliography

- Budhbhushanam - Chhatrapati Sambhaji Maharaj
- Chhatrapati Sambhaji Maharaj - V. S. Bendre
- Shivputra Sambhaji – Dr. Kamal Gokhale
- Ranzunjhaar – Dr. Sadashiv Shivade
- Mi Mrutunjay Mi Sambhaji – Sanjay Sonwani
- Jwaljwalantejas Sambhajiraja – Dr. Sadashiv Shivade
- Marathyanche Swatantra yudha – Dr. Jaysingrao Pawar
- Jedhe Shakavali – Dr. A. R. Kulkarni
- History of Aurangzeb – Jadunath Sarkar
- The Mughal-Maratha Relations – G. T. Kulkarni
- Bombay and the Siddis – D. R. Banaji
- House of Shivaji – Jadunath Sarkar
- Chhava – Shivaji Sawant
- Sambhaji – Vishwas Patil
- The English in Western India – Philip Anderson
- History of Marathas – S. G. Kolarkar
- An advanced history of India – R. C. Majumdar, H. C. Raychaudhari, Kalikinkar Datta
- Maratha Portuguese Relations – A. D. Pisurlekar

About Author

Mr. Sujit Namdev Tambe

Born: 30th July 1995

Mr. Sujit Tambe is Faculty, Author, and Corporate Trainer. He is young history Narrator of Chhatrapati Shivaji Maharaj & Dharmaveer Chhatrapati Sambhaji Mahraj. He has completed his B.E Mechanical, Diploma (Metallurgy), and M.B.A in HR. He is an Educationalist with Corporate Experience. He has conducted corporate training programs on varied topics like How to overcome depression & get self-motivated in daily life, Management learning's from Chhatrapati Shivaji Maharaj, Laws for medical practitioners, etc.

He has been rewarded an award named as "Veer Shivchhatrapati Maharashtraratna 2024" for his literature work on Chhatrapati Shivaji Maharaj & Dharmaveer Chhatrapati Sambhaji Maharaj. He has subject expertise in Human Resource Management, Organizational Behavior, Basics of Marketing, Management Fundamentals, Legal topics in HR.

Published Books:

1. शिवछत्रपती: सूत्र विश्वाचं (Notion Press)
2. Medicolegal Services (Symbiosis Center for Distance Learning Institute)
3. कविता संग्रह (Notion Press)

Author Sujit Tambe accepting blessings from Chhatrapati
Udayanraje Bhosale for the book

Author Sujit Tambe accepting blessings from Yuvraj
Sambhajiraje Chhatrapati for the book

Author Sujit Tambe accepting blessings from Yuvraj
Sambhajiraje Chhatrapati for the book

Author Sujit Tambe accepting blessings from former
Maharashtra State Health Minister Dr. Tanaji Sawant for
the book